Studying Children

An Introduction to Research Methods

Ross Vasta

State University of New York College at Brockport

W. H. Freeman and Company
San Francisco

Sponsoring Editor: W. Hayward Rogers; *Project Editor,* Nancy Flight; *Copyeditor:* Larry Olsen; *Designer:* Gary A. Head; *Illustration Coordinator:* Cheryl Nufer; *Artist:* Chuck Alessio; *Compositor:* Lienett Graphics; *Printer and Binder:* The Maple-Vail Book Manufacturing Group.

Library of Congress Cataloging in Publication Data

Vasta, Ross.
  Studying children.

  (A Series of books in psychology)
  Includes bibliographies and indexes.
  1. Child psychology—Methodology. 2. Child
psychology—Research. I. Title.
BF722.V37   155.4'072   78-25941
ISBN 0-7167-1067-6
ISBN 0-7167-1068-4 pbk.

Printed in the United States of America

3 4 5 6 7 8 9 MP 0 8 9 8 7 6 5 4 3 2

1985

Studying Children

A Series of Books in Psychology

Editors:

Jonathan Freedman
Gardner Lindzey
Richard F. Thompson

This project was conceived at Journey's End and is warmly dedicated to our Poquott friends (Mary, Allen, Rick, Gary, Denise, Brian, Monroe, etc.).

Contents

Preface   ix

PART I   **Scientific Inquiry**

Chapter **1**   The Scientific Method   3
Chapter **2**   Experimentation   15
Chapter **3**   Types of Research   32

PART II   **Basic Research Designs**

Chapter **4**   Longitudinal Research   51
Chapter **5**   Experimental Research   66
Chapter **6**   Time-Series Research   83

PART III   **Tactics of Investigation**

Chapter **7**   Basic Measures of Behavior   103
Chapter **8**   Complex Measures and Techniques   119
Chapter **9**   Techniques with Infants   139
Chapter **10**   Observational Methods   159

PART IV   Related Issues

Chapter **11** Ethical Considerations   187
Chapter **12** Scientific Communication   200

Name Index   207

Subject Index   210

Preface

Studying Children has grown from my experiences in teaching developmental psychology to undergraduates and in coauthoring a textbook on child development. Because developmental psychology is relatively young and is growing at a rapid pace, I have found myself continually struggling with the selection of the most useful instructional materials. An instructor must fulfill many conflicting needs in order to present an effective course in this subject: the need to be up to date but not to ignore the classics, the need to present a coherent world view but to represent all schools of thought, the need to consider theories but to respect empirical information in its own right.

My resolution of these conflicts is represented to some degree by this text. I have gradually become convinced that the most important knowledge we can give our students is *how to approach the discipline.* True, we must teach facts, but facts are changing so quickly that what we say today may well be inaccurate tomorrow. We also must teach theory, but theories are only as good as the evidence that supports them, and they too often have an ephemeral quality. What we can teach with a modicum of timelessness, however, is how child researchers go about the business of studying children. What types of questions do they ask? What methods do they use to address these questions? And what assumptions or probabilistic risks are involved in drawing their conclusions? This sort of knowledge may enable the student to evaluate new facts or theories as they emerge and thus to weather the rapid advances that surely will continue in this subject in the near future.

Unfortunately, most child psychology texts devote only one chapter (or less) to this important area. This book, therefore, is designed primarily as a supplement to such texts for introductory child development or developmental psychology courses. The material is presented at an elementary level, with no prerequisite psychology courses assumed. It also is brief enough to be used with a major text in a one-semester course.

In presenting child research methods, I have attempted to accomplish two goals: (1) to describe those aspects of psychological research common to all disciplines—the scientific method, the principles of experimentation, the major types of research design, and so on; and (2) to indicate some of the unique characteristics of research with children, including the various theoretical perspectives, many specific research techniques, and the important ethical considerations. For this reason, the text progresses from a general approach to specific procedures. Throughout the chapters, however, I have attempted to supply numerous examples of research with children to illustrate all levels of analysis. These examples are drawn from the entire age range (infancy to adolescence), they represent most current theoretical traditions (cognitive, behavioral, and so on), and they exemplify various research orientations (such as experimental child, developmental, and applied behavior analysis).

In some cases I have generated hypothetical studies and data, but in later chapters my illustrations of methodological issues involve actual published research reports. These were selected, again, to reflect the diversity of the subject and to acquaint the student with a number of reasonably well known and important investigations.

I am indebted to a number of individuals for their assistance and cooperation. Paul Mussen, Joan Grusec, Jerry Martin, Eleanor Willemsen, and Ronald Slaby offered comments and suggestions on an earlier version of this manuscript. Their remarks were excellent and of great value to me. I would also like to thank two student reviewers, Bonnie Kwiatkowski and Phil Copitch, for their suggestions. My typists, Debbie Sitterly, Barb Nicoll, and Pris McAllister, did an outstanding job under considerable pressure. The children and staff of the Brockport Campus School have been very cooperative in all my interactions with them, and their cooperation certainly contributed to my decision to write this text. I would especially like to thank Susan Marie Heiman, who assisted on technical aspects of the manuscript. Finally, I would like to express greatest appreciation to my wife, Linda, for her patience, tolerance, and supportive efforts.

December 1978   *Ross Vasta*

I

Scientific Inquiry

1 The Scientific Method

The study of children has occurred in one form or another for thousands of years. Philosophers, religious scholars, and early educators have all offered explanations of child behavior based on informal observations and recordings. It is only in the past century, however, that a truly systematic approach to this effort has been attempted. Only with the emergence of psychology as a separate scientific discipline in the late nineteenth century did the study of children begin to acquire an objective, orderly character.

Child psychology may be defined as the study of children's behavior and development. This statement appears simple enough, but it actually involves a number of important unwritten assumptions. These assumptions specify (1) acceptable methods of study, (2) a uniform language for reporting the information gathered, and (3) a set of rules for determining the value of that information. Taken together, these three assumptions comprise a set of rules, language, and procedures called the *scientific method*, which can be used to investigate almost any problem, issue, or phenomenon. In many fields of endeavor—such as psychology, medicine, and industry—the scientific approach has become almost universally accepted as the preferred method of investigation.

Several aspects of the scientific method set it apart from more informal ways of studying human behavior and shall be considered in some detail in this chapter. The study of humans, and of children in particular, poses a number of unique problems in the application of the scientific approach; these problems shall be taken up in later chapters. As we proceed, however, it is important to keep in mind that science represents only one way of describing and studying our world and that various other legitimate approaches may be taken.

Our discussion will necessarily begin at a rather abstract level, with the introduction of general concepts and ideas. In later chapters, these ideas shall gradually be tied more closely to specific techniques and procedures of research with children.

Theory

One of the fundamental concepts in science is the *theory*. In psychology, theories usually consist of a set of statements describing the relationship between human behavior and the factors that affect or explain it. Those statements which are supported by a good deal of scientific evidence are referred to as *laws*. When a statement is based primarily on the psychologist's ideas and has little or inconclusive support, it is called a *hypothesis*.

The important role of theory in science is to help guide the investigator's research. Sometimes a theory may indicate where more information needs to be obtained or what kinds of additional questions may require attention. As scientific data are gathered, they may support the psychologist's hypotheses or they may prove inconsistent with them. In the latter case, the researcher must then decide whether to alter the theory, collect additional information, or engage in some combination of the two.

Not all psychological research is designed to test theories, as we shall see in Chapter 3. And in fact some psychologists prefer to avoid complex theorizing as much as possible. Whether guided by theory or not, however, the collection of scientific evidence demands a number of important considerations.

Objectivity

One of the most important aspects of the scientific method is the emphasis on *objectivity*. In contrast to other approaches, where subjective experience, individual taste, or personal reactions might be sought, science attempts to deal with events whose occurrence, in principle, can be agreed upon by anyone. This is accomplished, in part, by establishing two criteria for any event or behavior that is to be investigated and analyzed.

1. *Events must be observable.* This criterion means simply that the event or behavior must be capable of observation by more than one person. We sometimes refer to such events as *public.** In psychology, the emphasis is on studying observable environmental events. This approach is used to guarantee that only agreed-upon, objective information will be gathered and considered.

At times, however, unobservable internal processes also may be of interest to the psychologist. Such processes as "fear" or "creativity" cannot actually be observed, although we often witness their *effects* in a person's behavior. These unobservable internal processes are called *hypothetical constructs;* they cannot be observed directly, but the psychologist may have reason to believe that they are an important determinant of a person's behavior. Rather than rejecting these processes because they cannot be observed, the scientist may decide to study *operational definitions* of these constructs. That is, the scientist would study those observable behaviors assumed to be related to, or to occur as a result of, the theoretical internal process. For example, a psychologist might operationally define "fear" as a group of specific emotional and withdrawal behaviors (crying, clinging to mother, hiding, and so on); likewise, he might operationalize "creativity" as a particular form of relationship between various behaviors (for example, the number of different colors or shapes a child

---

*A related concept is the *private event*—a psychological event that is observable only to a single person (e.g., a hallucination or a stomach ache). This form of observation is rarely used with children, however, and need not be pursued in detail.

uses in a drawing). Now, by examining these observable behaviors in relation to other environmental events, the psychologist can acquire information regarding the nature or functions of the internal processes. But such theoretical ideas must always be tested and verified by again examining observable behaviors.

2. *Events must be measurable.* The emphasis here is on defining events or behaviors in such a way that they can be easily specified and recorded. The use of automatic instrumentation frequently solves this problem. But when human observations are involved, the situation becomes much more complex. Two individuals may witness the identical observable event, but, as a result of previous experiences, prior expectations, or other such factors, they may describe the event very differently. To help eliminate this problem, psychologists always try to use only well-specified definitions. The complexity of human behavior, however, often makes this task quite difficult.

For example, developmental psychologists wishing to study the causes of children's aggression must take care to define that behavior very specifically. Should verbal comments be included? Should unsuccessful attempts at aggression be included? What is the basic unit of measurement —number of aggressive behaviors, intensity of aggressive assaults, time spent engaging in aggression? Often it is necessary to use a number of observers and compare their results, using specific rules for determining whether observational distortions have occurred. We shall examine this issue in more detail in Chapter 10.

These two criteria, observability and measurability, determine what is and is not permissible to include in a scientific analysis. Given that operational definitions permit the study of many unobservable processes, and considering the rapid advances in observational technology, the number of phenomena lying outside of the scientific method is quickly decreasing. Therefore, the fact that a phenomenon may not be currently within the realm of scientific analysis does not necessarily deny its existence or importance. Perhaps it only postpones its investigation until some future time.

The Nature of
Scientific Explanation

The scientific study of children has appeared to have two somewhat different goals: to *describe* behavior and development and to *explain* them. These two goals actually are not as distinct as they may seem, but to understand this we must first consider what the scientist means by the term *explanation*.

Types of Explanations

When a psychologist claims to understand behavior, or to explain it, this means that the *determinants* (causes) of that behavior have been identified. The two methods used to confirm the explanation are *prediction* and *control*. If the determinants of the behavior are actually known, the scientist should be able to predict the occurrence or nonoccurrence of the behavior by noting whether the necessary conditions exist. Likewise, the scientist should be able to control the occurrence or nonoccurrence of the behavior by presenting or removing the necessary conditions. When these criteria are met, the scientist has explained the behavior according to the requirements of the scientific method.

This definition of explanation may be somewhat at odds with our everyday definition of the word. Frequently we explain phenomena simply by appealing to a lower level of analysis. We explain the taste of great wine by describing its ingredients; we explain the success of the ingredients by considering their biological nature; we explain their biological nature by describing particular chemical reactions; we explain these chemical reactions by appealing to their molecular structure. This approach to explanation, known as *reductionism*, was quite popular in the early years of psychology. But the modern study of behavior more frequently involves explanations of phenomena at a single level of analysis. That is, when we study the world from a psychological perspective, we focus primarily on *psychological events*. These are any events that an individual can be shown to respond to or interact with. Sights, sounds, bodily sensations, images, and emotions are all potentially legitimate events in psychological investigation. Internal physiological structures or mechanisms, however, usually do not fit this definition. For example, neuronal flexion of the leg muscles is one obvious "cause" of running, but it would not be considered a psychological determinant of a child's fleeing from a stranger.

A related issue concerns a form of explanation known as *teleology*. Determinants of events always precede or occur simultaneously with the behavior they cause; they can never exist in the future.* It may often appear that we perform a given behavior in order to achieve some goal. But the causes of such behavior actually reside in our previous experiences with similar situations, as well as in the current circumstances surrounding the behavior. When we say that a child "runs away in order to avoid punishment" or "acts up so that he will get attention," we are proposing teleological explanations for the behavior. Such cause-and-effect statements are not considered appropriate in modern scientific analysis, as we shall see in the next section.

Determinants of Behavior

The determinants of human behavior can be classified into three categories. The first category consists of *historical* determinants. Each individual behavior probably has a reasonably long history (even infants' behaviors probably are subject to some influences in this category). Historical determinants frequently involve learning or conditioning processes. The particular behavior, or a similar one, may have occurred previously and produced positive or negative consequences; or it may have been associated with other important events or

---

*If you have taken an introductory psychology course, you may recall that *consequences* are an important determinant of behavior in operant conditioning. But consequences only affect *future* occurrences of the behavior, and, at that point, they would have become a historical determinant.

behaviors; or the form of the response may have changed as a result of repeatedly producing it. Although none of these factors may be present when the behavior is currently produced, they nevertheless may be important for understanding the behavior.

A second category of determinants involves *current situational* variables. Behavior does not occur in a vacuum but is always produced in the context of other environmental factors. These may include specific people, settings, time of day, immediately preceding events, and so on. Each of these variables, or their particular combination, may exert an important influence on the occurrence of the behavior.

Finally, to completely understand a behavior we must consider its *organismic* determinants. These are biological or physiological variables specific to the individual. They include the current state of the person (hungry, fatigued, agitated, and so on), the person's sensory capabilities, and the person's motor-skills capabilities. All these variables clearly play an important role in determining whether a given behavioral response will or will not occur.

Let us consider an example of the interaction of these sources of determinants. A child may look at a fruit tree and say "Look at the apple!" This seemingly simple behavior undoubtedly has determinants in each of the three categories just described. The child must previously have seen an apple to be able to recognize it and must previously have learned the name for this object to be able to say it. Some language learning was necessary for producing the comprehensible grammatical utterance. The occurrence of this verbal response also must certainly be a result of a specific situational factor—the presence of the apple. The nature of the remark additionally suggests that someone else is present to hear it. It further implies that the child's attention is drawn to that particular stimulus-object rather than to any other object in the immediate environment at that moment. Finally, the child must be capable of seeing the apple clearly enough to recognize it, and the child must be physiologically capable of producing the vocal response. The state of the child's appetite also might play some role in the likelihood of producing the comment.

This brief analysis should make it clear that explaining the causes of even very simple behavior can be a complex task. This is particularly true when the scientist must verify these determinants through appropriate prediction and control procedures. It should not be surprising, then, that the scientific approach to the study of human behavior requires a high degree of objectivity, precision, and rigorous adherence to agreed-upon procedures. Attempting to understand the behavior of children by casual observation may be adequate for some purposes, but explaining this behavior at the level demanded by the scientific method is quite another task.

Description Versus Explanation

We mentioned earlier that one apparent goal of psychology is to describe human behavior. Descriptive accounts, however, usually do not simply enumerate the behaviors, but they present them relative to other factors or environmental events. One of the most common of these factors is age. We may describe a child's language development by noting the forms of speech that are produced at different ages. Likewise, the development of motor skills is often described according to a timetable or age-progression.

Descriptive accounts of behavior are studied relative to other factors in addition to age. Social development, for example, is often investigated by observing the nature of the child's interactions with others and by noting the environmental circumstances surrounding the behavior. The study of parent-child relationships or peer-group interactions sometimes employs the same approach.

Examining behavior relative to other variables, however, is not an exclusive feature of *descriptive* analysis. We have seen that scientific *explanation* involves the identification of determinants of behavior at the same level of analysis. This can be restated to say that *behavior is explained by describing it relative to other factors or environmental events.* When restated in this fashion, differences between the two approaches virtually disappear.

There is no fundamental distinction, then, between the goals of description and explanation in modern psychology, although explanatory accounts are probably more complete. Perhaps the distinction has persisted because it is closely tied to another distinction involving research methods. Research conducted in naturalistic settings often appears to focus on describing phenomena, whereas research conducted in more formal laboratory settings seems to focus on explaining phenomena. We shall examine some of these basic distinctions in research methods in Chapter 3.

Constructs as Explanation

It is important at this point to consider a practice common in everyday life that is sometimes employed by psychologists as well. This practice is the use of hypothetical constructs as explanations of behavior. We suggested earlier that unobservable internal processes such as creativity can be studied by operationally defining them in terms of specific overt behaviors. But it is crucial to keep in mind that such constructs remain theoretical; that is, their existence is assumed, but has not been verified.

For example, we sometimes hear that "a child performed well on an IQ test because she is intelligent." In this case, the performance on the test is used as an operational definition of the construct "intelligence." But in this situation the construct is used to explain the behavior. The important question here is whether anything is gained by adding the construct to our analysis of the behavior under study. If we can identify the determinants of the child's behavior from her past history, present circumstances, and individual organismic characteristics, does the "intelligence" construct provide any additional information to our understanding of this behavior? The principal test of the value of any construct is its *scientific utility*. That is, does the construct improve our ability to explain—to predict and control—behavior? If a hypothetical construct such as "intelligence" increases our ability to predict a large number of different behaviors by individuals of various ages in a variety of situations, psychologists may choose to retain the construct as an important part of their theoretical analysis of behavior. But if the construct offers little that is new, its utility would be questionable, and it would probably be abandoned.

Some psychologists adhere strictly to the philosophy of explaining behavior in terms of observable events, and they prefer to avoid using internal constructs as determinants of behavior. These psychologists may sometimes use the construct name (for example, "intelligence") simply as a descriptive label for organizing a set of behaviors possessing some common feature. But it is not necessarily assumed that all of the separate behaviors have a common set of determinants. Either of these approaches is legitimate, and there is no need for us to choose between them at this point.

Testability

In addition to requiring objectivity, the scientific method also requires that any useful theory or hypothesis be testable. This means that a theory must be stated in such a way that specific predictions can be made and tested by observable events. If a theory appears to explain a phenomenon, but its hypotheses can never be put to a reasonable test, its value to the scientist is quite limited.

For example, suppose a developmental psychologist proposed that children engage in fantasy play because someone in their family history had previously had those actual experiences. This theory may account for the child's current behavior, but we cannot subject it to the usual scientific tests. We cannot examine its predictability, because it merely suggests that some individual's current behavior may one day appear in their yet-unborn relative's fantasy play. And we cannot test it by systematically presenting and removing the suspected determinant, because we do not know which current experience to alter and which later fantasy behaviors to observe. This theory accounts for the phenomenon of fantasy play, but the scientist has no method of testing it. Thus, it has no scientific utility.

TABLE 1.1
The Scientific Method

Objectivity

Events must be observable, or involve operational definitions.

Events must be measurable.

Testability

Theories must be testable and capable of being disproved.

Theories are never proved; they are only supported with some degree of certainty.

Explanation

Behavior is explained by identifying determinants at the same level of analysis.

Determinants are psychological events, including historical, situational, and organismic factors.

The value of a hypothetical construct is its ability to improve prediction and control of behavior.

The process of theory-testing has other important aspects as well. When a psychologist sets out to test a hypothesis (a specific prediction derived from the larger theory), it is not assumed that the prediction will be proved. Rather, science deals with *levels of certainty*. To test the hypothesis that infants smile less in the presence of strangers, a psychologist might set up a controlled situation, where a number of eight-week-old infants are systematically exposed to familiar and unfamiliar people, and observe the infants' responses. Even if the psychologist were to find that all the infants smiled less in the presence of each stranger, it could not be asserted that the relationship between smiling and familiarity had been proved. At best, the psychologist could claim that the data *supported* or were *consistent with* the hypothesis. The only way absolute proof of the relationship could ever be established would be to test all infants with all strangers. This requirement may appear somewhat absurd, and the data of the sample may appear sufficient to confirm the prediction, but this point actually is the basis of a very important characteristic of the scientific method.

Rarely would any experiment yield results as clear as our example. More likely, data supporting the hypothesis would have shown most of the infants smiling less often at most of the strangers. In this event, we must make some decision as to whether the evidence is adequate to accept or reject the psychologist's prediction. The rules that are used to make such decisions are provided by *inferential statistical methods*. We shall not pursue this topic until later chapters, but it will be obvious as we proceed with other topics that, in experimental research, proof is elusive, and even relative certainty is often the subject of much debate.

Conclusion

We have begun at a very general level by presenting the basic assumptions of the scientific method. These fundamental ideas form the basis of later chapters and should be considered carefully. At times, the methods and assumptions of science may involve very different ways of looking at and talking about our world than we have previously encountered. It is important, then, to try to maintain this perspective as we proceed through the book. We mentioned earlier that the scientific method is only one way of approaching events—but it is a very consistent method and has proved enormously useful in many areas of research.

In addition, science often seems to require learning a new language, and a good deal of new terminology has already been introduced. A good deal more is to come. It may prove worthwhile to review these terms before proceeding, because they will be encountered again in later chapters. In the next chapter we shall expand our focus from the underlying assumptions of the scientific method to an outline of the experimental method.

2 Experimentation

The heart of the scientific method is the experiment. Psychologists employ other methods of research, such as naturalistic observational techniques, but the experiment is clearly the most popular and useful research approach. We begin by considering only the basic framework of the experimental method, postponing discussion of more specific designs and techniques until later chapters.

Determining Cause and Effect

We have seen that behavior is explained by identifying its determinants using prediction and control procedures. In simple terms, the scientist tries to make sense of the many changes in behavior (and other events) that are continually occurring around us. This can be accomplished, in part, through experimental procedures to determine which events are the *causes* of other events (*effects*).

Functional Analysis

The psychological experiment is designed to establish *functional relationships* between environmental events and behavior. The events are called *independent variables*. They are "variable" because each may assume at least two different levels (values) along a dimension. Temperature is an environmental variable because it can assume many different levels along a particular scale. Food is an environmental variable, because its amount, type, or form can be systematically varied along any of these dimensions. Events are "independent" because the psychologist is free to use any level or combination of levels in the experimental situation. This planned variation is referred to as *experimental manipulation* of the independent variable.

The behavior under study is called the *dependent variable*. Its "variability," or different levels of occurrence, is studied in relation to the various levels of the independent variable. That is, the different levels of behavior produced at each level of the environmental event indicate the strength of the relationship between the two variables. The behavior is called "dependent" because any changes observed in it are a result of (depend on) the environmental event. Thus, the psychologist *independently* manipulates events, and the behavior *dependently* changes as a result.

The individuals studied in an experiment are called the *subjects* of the research. An important requirement of the experimental method is that the group of subjects exposed to each *treatment condition* (level of the independent variable) be initially equivalent. To put it another way, the only difference between the various groups of subjects should be the nature of the experimental manipulation that they receive. In this way, any later differences in behavior among the groups can confidently be attributed to the effects of the different levels of the independent variable.

A procedure that is frequently used for accomplishing this equivalence is *random assignment* of subjects to treatment conditions. In this procedure, each subject is randomly (unsystematically) placed in one of the experimental conditions by using such methods as flipping a coin or consulting a table of random numbers. The use of this randomization procedure is based on the knowledge that no two subjects in any study are ever completely identical. Rather, each subject possesses a unique combination of different characteristics, both physical (height, weight, genetic makeup, and so on) and historical (age, previous experiences, prior learning, and so on). The psychologist may attempt to ensure that subjects in each condition are equivalent on one or more of these characteristics (such as age or sex), but ultimately it is impossible to create groups that are precisely matched on every characteristic. Therefore, the psychologist relies on the randomization process, assuming that in the long run the many different characteristics are likely to balance out among the groups as more subjects are randomly added to each group. It follows that our confidence in randomization increases as the number of subjects in each group increases. (A second subject-selection procedure, *matching*, will be discussed in Chapter 5.)

An exception to the random-assignment procedure occurs when a subject characteristic is the independent variable of interest. For example, a psychologist may wish to determine performance differences on a particular task in males versus females, or two-year-olds versus five-year-olds, or good readers versus poor readers. It is, of course, not possible to assign a child to such a condition randomly, because the particular subject and level of the variable are inseparable. We call such variables *nonmanipulable* independent variables. Studies involving this type of independent variable are not "true" experiments, since cause-and-effect relationships cannot be established as clearly. That is, because we cannot assign a subject to a condition randomly, there is a somewhat greater likelihood that our treatment groups may differ systematically in other ways as well. For example, if we wished to compare good and poor readers on a particular dependent measure, it might be that our two groups differed in other important ways. The good readers might come from better-educated parents or a better socioeconomic background, or they might display more sophisticated cognitive abilities in general. Any differences observed between the groups might have several possible explanations. For this reason, studies involving nonmanipulable independent variables are referred to as *quasi-experimental designs* (Campbell and Stanley, 1966). For the most part, such studies are conducted and analyzed in the same manner as true experiments. However, we must be somewhat more cautious in interpreting any results obtained by this method.

A Hypothetical Experiment

To illustrate the relationship between an independent and a dependent variable, let us consider an example. A psychologist interested in children's prosocial behavior decides to test the hypothesis that a functional relationship exists between how a child obtains a reward (pennies) and the child's willingness to share the reward with other children. Three levels of the independent variable (source of reward) are studied: (1) reward obtained by performing a difficult task. (2) reward obtained by performing an easy task, and (3) reward obtained freely. In this study, the dependent variable (sharing) is defined as the number of pennies donated to a charity for needy children. Twenty third-grade children are randomly assigned to each of the three treatment conditions.

For the moment, we shall not consider many of the procedural details or problems. Let us simply assume that the psychologist observes (and inferential statistics confirm) that children donate the least money when the reward required a difficult task, somewhat more money when the reward required an easy task, and the most money when the reward was provided for no effort. The psychologist can claim to have demonstrated a relationship between an independent variable and a dependent variable. In this case, it would be legitimate to conclude that *children's sharing is a function of the source of reward.*

The phrase "a function of" is borrowed from mathematics and merely implies that as one variable (independent) changes over some range, a related variable (dependent) also changes in a predictable manner. This approach to experimentation, involving the identification of functional relationships between independent variables and behaviors, is referred to as a *functional analysis of behavior.*

It must be emphasized that the conclusion drawn in our example does not imply that the source of reward is the only variable affecting the children's sharing. As we saw in Chapter 1, the determinants of this and any other behavior probably are numerous and perhaps quite complex. But, by systematically establishing these functional relationships, the principal causes

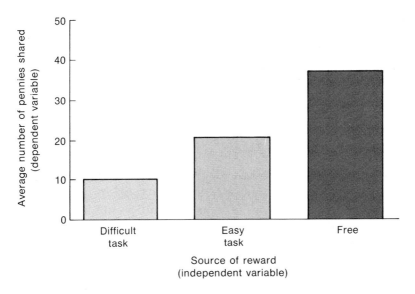

FIGURE 2.1
Graph illustrating the results of a hypothetical experiment. Bars represent the average number of pennies shared by children in each of three experimental conditions.

of the behavior are gradually identified—that is, the behavior is explained.

The results of this experiment may be presented graphically, as illustrated in Figure 2.1. The behavior under study (dependent variable) is usually presented on the vertical axis, and the different levels of the independent variable are presented on the horizontal axis. In this case, the data represent the average number of pennies donated by the twenty children in each of the three experimental conditions (see Long and Lerner, 1974, for actual research on this question).

Hypothesis Testing

What conclusion could we have reached if the children's sharing had not varied with the different sources of reward? Actually, nothing very definite. We could only have asserted that, in this study, sharing was not a function of source of reward. We could not claim to have proved this nonrelation-ship, because all possible situations had not been examined. But it is important to consider why we could not make the same type of statement that we did when the relationship was supported.

Psychological experiments are always designed to study *changes* or *differences* among events and behaviors. An *experimental hypothesis,* such as the one in our example, always predicts differences in a specific behavior as a function of changes in a specific independent variable. In any study, there is, in addition, always an alternative hypothesis, which predicts that no differences in behavior will be observed at the different levels of the independent variable. This *null hypothesis,* in principle, is built into every experiment.

When the experimental hypothesis is supported (differences in behavior are observed corresponding to different levels of the independent variable), inferential statistics can permit us to reject the null hypothesis and to conclude, with a reasonable degree of certainty, that a functional relationship has been identified. That is, we can accept the experimental hypothesis. But when major differences in behavior are not observed, our statistical methods are designed to permit us only to reject the experimental hypothesis—we cannot make any conclusions with any certainty regarding the null hypothesis. To put it simply, *we can never accept the null hypothesis that a behavior and an independent variable are unrelated.*

The statistical basis for this assumption is well beyond the scope of this book. But it may be useful to think of psychological experimentation simply as a one-way process. The experimental hypothesis (prediction of differences) can be either accepted or rejected, but the null hypothesis (prediction of no differences) can only be rejected. As we proceed with later topics, it should become clear why this unbalanced approach is necessary and useful.

Sources of Bias

When an independent variable is presented along a range of values and a behavior changes in a corresponding manner, we can conclude, *with some degree of certainty*, that a functional relationship between the two exists. But there are also a large number of factors that may contribute to the remaining uncertainty. Some of these other factors would lead to conclusions other than the one suggested by the outcome of the experiment. That is, the observed changes in the behavior may have been a result of something other than the experimental variation of the independent variable. We refer to these factors as *biasing influences*.

To increase the degree of certainty that the psychologist will have in the observed results, it is necessary to plan in advance *to control for* these other factors. Two principal ways of accomplishing such experimental control are to (1) eliminate the other factors, or (2) arrange to study them in addition to the major variables of interest. Often these two control techniques are both used in a single study. The specific control procedures selected for use depend on many characteristics of the research. We shall consider these in more detail later. In this section, only a few of the most common factors requiring experimental controls will be examined.

Sampling Bias

In most experiments, the observations made on a group of subjects are used to draw conclusions regarding a much larger population. If the group of experimental subjects is somehow very different from the remainder of the population, the conclusions may prove to be quite inaccurate. Therefore, the procedures used to select the experimental subjects must ensure that a representative group is investigated. When subjects are selected from a larger population, we say that they are *sampled* from the population. The population can be very large (for example, all the children in California) or very small (all the babies born at a local hospital last Tuesday). The problem to be avoided is known as *sampling bias*, a situation where the experimental sample differs from the larger population in any important aspect.

For example, a psychologist decides to investigate the degree to which attitudes of adolescent males are influenced by the opinions of others. Specifically, the psychologist wishes to determine whether adolescents' attitudes toward premarital sexual relations are influenced more by the opinion of someone similar to themselves or by the opinion of someone regarded as an expert. To examine this question, the investigator plans to have the subjects read a passage promoting the value of premarital relations and then to fill out a questionnaire to express their own viewpoint. One group of subjects will be told that the passage was written by a student at a nearby school, a second group will be told that it was written by a clinical psychologist, and a third group will not be given any information regarding the author's identity.

The population under study is described simply as twelve- to fifteen-year-old males in New England. The psychologist decides to select the experimental sample by studying thirty individuals (ten in each condition) at a randomly selected junior high school in each of four different counties of Connecticut, Massachusetts, and Vermont. The actual sampling procedure involves going to the school at the end of the day and testing male subjects at random as they leave.

Unfortunately, the psychologist fails to take into account two factors common to most of these schools: (1) many males on athletic teams have to practice immediately after school and do not leave until much later, and (2) males leaving with females are much less likely to take the time to fill out the questionnaire. Without intending to, the psychologist has excluded two segments of the population of interest from the experimental sample: "jocks" and "lovers." Because the issue involves male-female relationships, it is reasonable to expect the initial attitudes of these two groups to differ considerably from those of the rest of the population. To put it another way, the psychologist's experimental sample may be very much unlike the larger population under study. The sampling bias in this experiment greatly reduces the representativeness of the sample, thereby making conclusions regarding the larger population of adolescent males in New England very questionable.

One of the most common methods of sampling a representative group of subjects from a population involves *independent random sampling*. In this procedure, the selection of each subject has no effect on the likelihood of the selection of any other subject (independent), and the initial probability of being selected is the same for everyone in the population (random). In this example, each individual did not have an equal chance of being included in the sample because the "jocks" were much less available and the "lovers" were much less willing to participate.

Of course, we cannot be sure that the biased sample actually would have produced results different from a more appropriate sample. And in fact, no sample will ever be perfectly representative of the population from which it was drawn, although larger samples usually come closer to achieving this goal. But the experimental method demands that we select our experimental subjects as carefully and in as unbiased a manner as possible.

A particular form of sampling bias, known as *cohort effects*, is evident in some kinds of developmental research. When a developmental psychologist wishes to investigate changes in a behavior over a range of ages, one method would be to study the subjects when they are young and to continue to study them as they grow older. This approach, however, would be quite time-consuming. A much easier method would be simply to study a group of individuals of different ages at the same time.

For example, one could examine cognitive skills at various ages by comparing the performances of subjects who were five, twelve, twenty, and fifty years of age. If differences were observed as a function of the age of the subject (independent variable), a conclusion might be drawn regarding the relationship of age to cognitive performance.

The problem with this approach is that the individuals under study differ not only in age but in another important characteristic—generation. In this particular experiment, differences in generations may be reflected, for example, in very different educational experiences. The fifty-year-old subjects were born and raised during the Depression, when the amount and quality of education were probably quite low. The twenty-year-olds were born just after Sputnik, when the space-race stimulated an emphasis on scientific and math-

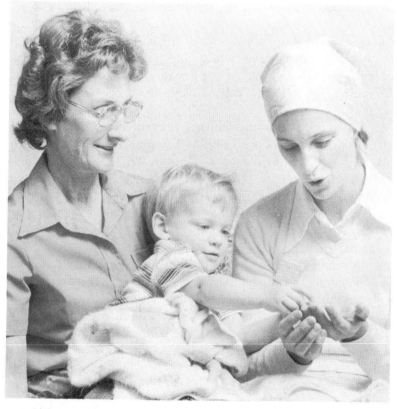

FIGURE 2.2
Studying individuals of different ages requires careful consideration of possible *cohort effects*—in this case, the fact that each person is a member of a different generation. (Photograph by Emilio A. Mercado.)

ematical skills. The twelve-year-old subjects are products of the late 1960s, which generated an increasing concern for the social and emotional development of the child.

The important point here is that much more may be involved in studying individuals of different ages than simply the number of years they have lived. That is, we cannot be sure in our study that the performance of the five-year-olds, for example, is comparable to what the other groups would have displayed at the same age. We shall return to this issue when we compare longitudinal and cross-sectional research methods (see Baltes and Schaie, 1974, for a discussion of this problem in relation to IQ scores).

Reactivity

Once the subjects of the research have been appropriately selected, we may turn our attention to sources of bias in the experimental procedures. As in the example presented earlier in the chapter, much research involves exposing subjects to some combination of independent variables and observing and measuring a dependent variable. The experimenter hopes to be able to conclude that the observed variations in the behavior of interest are a result of the specific variables being manipulated. But changes in the behavior of interest sometimes result from a process called *experimental reactivity*—that is, changes in behavior caused by the experimenter's observation or measurement techniques.

There are three principal types of reactivity: changes in behavior which occur (1) during simple observation, (2) as a result of repeated assessment, or (3) in response to variation in virtually any environmental variable. These three types are very much interrelated, but we shall examine them separately in the situations where they most often are a problem.

The first type of reactivity is frequently troublesome when an experimenter is collecting data in a naturalistic setting, and the subjects are aware of the observations. For example, a school psychologist wishes to examine the effects of class size (independent variable) on teachers' attention to individual students (dependent variable) and decides to attend several different-sized classes to observe teacher-child interactions. Somewhat unexpectedly, the psychologist observes that a high degree of attention is given to individual children regardless of the number of class members. Being somewhat suspicious of this conclusion, the psychologist arranges to reobserve these same classes without the teachers' awareness of the observations (perhaps using a hidden videotape camera). This time, the anticipated relationship is observed: teacher attention decreases as class size increases. In this case, the teachers' attention was normally a function of the number of students, but the initial attempts to observe that relationship had a reactive effect—the behavior under study was temporarily altered by the observation process.

The simplest method of dealing with this type of reactivity is the use of *unobtrusive measures*. That is, as the psychologist in our example discovered, measurement procedures that do not involve the subjects' awareness often provide a more accurate picture of the behavior under study. In Chapter 10 we shall examine other solutions to this problem, and in Chapter 11 we shall discuss the ethical aspects of such a procedure.

A second type of reactivity involves the effects of repeated performance of a task used to assess the dependent variable. A psychologist interested in children's spatial-relations abilities wishes to determine whether training in visual-scanning will improve performance. The procedure involves testing the subjects on a spatial-relations test to determine their initial level of performance, and then training them for four weeks in visual-scanning. Each week the spatial-relations test is readministered to monitor any improvement resulting from the training. At the end of the four-week experiment, the children perform much better on the spatial-relations test than they had originally.

These results appear to demonstrate that the visual-scanning training improved test performance. To check this conclusion, however, the psychologist decides to test another group of subjects on the spatial-relations test once every four weeks without any intervening training. After the five administrations of the test, these subjects show the same amount of improvement as the others. In this case the multiple-testing procedure was reactive, because the children's performance improved simply as a result of practice with the spatial-relations test.

One way to eliminate this kind of problem would be to use several different forms of the dependent variable, such as five spatial-relations tests, each made up of different problems. This procedure is often difficult or undesirable, however, and it may be better simply to study the "practice" variable rather than try to eliminate it. This could be accomplished by including a *control group* of subjects, who receive only the test without the training, and comparing their results with those of an *experimental group*. Unless the performance of the experimental subjects improves more than that of the control subjects, no functional relationship between the independent variable (training) and the dependent variable (spatial-relations) can be claimed.

The third type of reactivity is sometimes referred to as the *Hawthorne effect*. In 1939, a dramatic finding was reported from the Hawthorne, Massachusetts, plant of the Western Electric Company (Roethlisberger and Dickson, 1939). Investigators were interested in identifying variables that might affect the rate of workers' production. To study this question, the experimenters systematically varied environmental conditions, such as light, temperature, and work hours, and observed the resulting effects on production. Quite surprisingly, virtually every manipulation—raising temperature, lowering temperature, increasing light, reducing light, and so on—had the effect of increasing production rates.

It is unlikely that the observed changes in the workers' production were the result of manipulation of these independent variables. Rather, the subjects' awareness of being studied seemed to have a reactive influence on their behavior, perhaps resulting simply from the increased attention accompanying every manipulation. Whenever human beings are the subject of experimentation, this potential problem must be addressed.

The two procedures used to remedy the other types of reactivity can also apply here. Subtle manipulation of the independent variables plus unobtrusive observation of the dependent behaviors is one alternative. A better approach might be to include a group of control subjects, who receive only an "attention" manipulation, and compare their performance with that of the experimental group receiving the independent variable of interest. This type of reactivity is probably short-lived; the influence of increased attention tends to diminish with time. Thus the use of an extended period of observation is also useful in dealing with such reactivity.

Maturation and History

Experimental procedures often involve initial testing of a behavior (*pretesting*), introduction of the independent variable, and retesting of the behavior (*posttesting*). The differences in results between the pretests and the posttests indicate the effects of the independent variable. But other events may occur during this period and may contribute to the behavior change.

One type of event involves biological or physiological changes in the organism under study. In humans, this is typically a problem only in infancy research, where such *maturational* factors occur rapidly, although long-term studies with older subjects are also open to this problem.

For example, a psychologist may be interested in studying the influence of the auditory environment on newborns' preferences for listening to the human voice. The psychologist uses a special apparatus whereby the infants' head-turning will control the sound source. If the infants turn their heads to the left, a tape recording of human voices is played; if they turn their heads to the right, animal (nonhuman) vocal sounds are played. The psychologist tests the infants at ten days of age and discovers that they have no particular listening preference— that is, they turn their heads equally often to the left and right. A two-week period of exposure to human voices is then introduced, during which three hours of human talking is presented to the infants each morning and evening. At the end of this experimental period, the infants are again tested for listening preference, and all are observed to prefer human voices.

The experimenter concludes that exposure to human voices increases infants' preferences for those sounds, but at least two alternative explanations of these results are possible. The initial testing may have indicated not a lack of preference for the human sounds, but simply underdeveloped auditory capabilities during the first days of life. Over the course of the two-week exposure, the infants' auditory abilities may have improved substantially, permitting a more accurate assessment of their listening preferences. Another explanation involves the infants' learning of the left-right discrimination

TABLE 2.1
Biasing Influences and Experimental Controls

Potential Source of Bias	Control Procedures
Biased sample	Independent random sampling
Effects of observation (reactivity)	Unobtrusive measures
Effects of repeated testing	Practice control group
Hawthorne effect	Attention control group
Effects of maturation	Pre-post control group
Historical events	Replication
Chance findings	Statistical verification; replication

necessary to indicate a preference. Because such learning capability seems to develop rapidly after birth, again the initial assessment may have been a poor measure of actual listening preference. Both of these alternative explanations imply that maturational development, rather than environmental stimulation, was responsible for the observed changes in behavior. Fortunately, controlling for such factors is usually not difficult. A second group of infants, who do not receive the intervening experimental manipulation, could be used to check for these same changes in behavior.

Sometimes nonmaturational events occur between pretesting and posttesting of a behavior and have unplanned influences on results. Psychologists studying changes in children's occupational preferences between kindergarten and first grade would do well to note the television heroes popular during that particular season. Investigations of changes in adolescent moral and political development should not be conducted without awareness of current political campaigns, elections, or social unrest. Such influences are sometimes difficult to control for, because the critical intervening events may not always be apparent. Conclusions based upon this type of longer-term research, then, must be considered very carefully.

Chance Findings

One additional type of bias, which may hinder firm experimental conclusions, is the role of chance findings. In any experiment, differences in performance between groups of subjects, or between pretests and posttests, conceivably could occur simply "by chance." This is possible because all behavior includes some *variability;* that is, it is not perfectly stable or predictable. Inferential statistics are used, therefore, to calculate the probability of differences occurring merely as a result of such chance variation. To standardize research findings, psychologists have required a level of certainty to be adopted before a cause-and-effect relationship can be concluded. Differences in results must be large enough so that the likelihood of their being a result of chance is less than five in one hundred. This standard is called the five percent confidence level.

There always remains the small possibility (five percent) that observed differences in results are not a function of the experimental manipulation. This is usually not seen as a problem requiring attention, because the five percent uncertainty level is considered a tolerable margin of error. Nevertheless, one way to increase our confidence in any functional relationship is through the process of *replication*. This simply means repeating the experiment in some manner. This can be done, for example, by conducting it again at another time and place. We shall see later that some research designs actually incorporate the replication process within the original procedures.

Conclusion

The scientific experiment is the most widely used method of establishing functional relationships between events and behaviors. Its popularity is based upon the rigor and specificity it brings to the investigatory process. But, again, in this chapter we have seen that such relationships are demonstrated only beyond some level of uncertainty. A few of the major factors contributing to this uncertainty were discussed, and a few general solutions were offered. As we continue, more specific problems and more specific procedural details will be considered.

Many of the examples used in this chapter deliberately included inadequate experimental controls. This was done for instructional purposes and should not be taken to suggest that much psychological research is poorly conducted. It is the case, however, that the basic information provided up to this point could be sufficient to allow the perceptive student to scrutinize a good deal of psychological experimentation for possible shortcomings. And, when the text is completed, it also may be possible to accomplish the more difficult task of designing and conducting original experimental research.

References

Baltes, P. B., and Schaie, K. W. Aging and I.Q.: The myth of the twilight years. *Psychology Today*, 1974, **7** (10). 35–40.

Campbell, D. T., and Stanley, J. C. *Experimental and quasi-experimental designs for research*. Chicago: Rand McNally, 1966.

Long, G. T., and Lerner, M. J. Deserving, the "personal contract," and altruistic behavior in children. *Journal of Personality and Social Psychology*, 1974, **29**, 551–556.

Roethlisberger, E. J., and Dickson, W. J. *Management and the worker*. Cambridge, Mass.: Harvard University Press, 1939.

3   Types of Research

The purpose of this text is to discuss various methods of studying children. It would be convenient if these methods could be easily classified into well-defined categories or clusters, but this is not the case. Some classification schemes are based upon the purpose of the research, others are based upon the methods employed, and some are even based upon the subject population under study. It would be very difficult to devise a single categorization scheme to include all of the possible combinations of these methods. We shall try, instead, simply to outline some of the major categories that have been used in the past and continue to be useful.

General Dimensions

All research may be considered to lie somewhere along two different dimensions—descriptive versus manipulative and basic versus applied. These labels do not represent discrete (completely separate) categories but are merely endpoints along a continuous scale.

Descriptive Versus Manipulative

We discussed this distinction to some degree when we considered the nature of scientific explanation. Descriptive research is often characterized by simple observational techniques, which sometimes involve the collection of very large amounts of data and which frequently are conducted in nonlaboratory settings. What distinguishes this method is that the researcher simply observes and records but does not intrude or interfere with the "natural" situation.

In contrast, manipulative research involves the experimental method, where the psychologist deliberately manipulates a variable and observes consequent changes in the behavior of interest. In this case, the experimenter does not simply wait for environmental variations to occur but produces them in a systematic, controlled fashion.

For example, one psychologist might go into a child's home and observe the variables that control the mother's various disciplinary techniques; another psychologist might bring the mother and child into the laboratory and systematically vary aspects of the situation while also observing the mother's disciplinary techniques. The first psychologist would be considered to use a descriptive method and the latter to use a manipulative method.

One potential distinction may be that the manipulative method focuses on what functional relationships *can exist* (if specific variables are manipulated), whereas the descriptive approach emphasizes the functional relationships that typically *do exist*. A related distinction is that descriptive research in any area often precedes manipulative research—that is, potential determining variables are identified in the natural setting and then carefully tested in the laboratory. Ultimately, the goals of these two methods are identical—to identify the determinants of the mother's behavior.

Applied Versus Basic

This dimension is based primarily upon the purpose of the research. Applied investigations are designed to solve a specific problem or to provide information that is immediately useful. Much of the research conducted on clinical issues and in education, for example, has as its goal the immediate application of its findings.

Basic research may be thought of as any investigation that is not of the applied type. When a psychologist attempts to explain some aspect of human behavior or understand a process or acquire knowledge about a phenomenon, the results are not expected to be immediately valuable for any specific use. The findings simply add to our store of information, and they may not become relevant to some real problem until much later.

For example, a psychologist investigating cognitive processes in children discovers that when new words are presented for the first time in a meaningful context rather than in isolation, they are learned much more quickly. This finding may have relevance to the psychologist's theoretical model of children's information-processing and thereby be considered basic research. An educational psychologist who becomes aware of these findings might immediately use them to develop a more efficient vocabulary-acquisition program and a new first-grade reader. Now the same information has acquired applied value. In the course of designing and testing the reader, however, the educational psychologist discovers that the ease of learning the new words seems also to be a function of the difficulty of the material in which they are presented. This relationship is relevant to appropriately designing other reading materials, but it also provides an important addition to the cognitive psychologist's theoretical model.

These examples illustrate simply that basic and applied research are often difficult to distinguish. They are typically labeled by the original purpose of the investigations, but their outcomes often do not correspond to these purposes. Again, the width of this dimension becomes narrower when we consider such interrelations of research findings and their potential applications both to theory and to practice.

Other dimensions could be considered, such as laboratory versus field studies, theoretical versus nontheoretical research, and single-subject versus group experiments. But these distinctions often are even less clear, and they do not make a major contribution to our understanding or development of research methods (see Reese and Lipsitt, 1970, for more on these various dimensions).

Research Perspectives

We turn now to five different ways of considering human behavior. These approaches are defined in part by the techniques of investigation that are employed and also by the particular kinds of issues that are addressed. Often they are used in combination.

Developmental

One of the most popular modes of investigation among child psychologists is the developmental approach. Here the psychologist examines changes in behavior over a period of development. The time-frame of interest can be brief, as in the developmental changes occurring during the first days after birth, or the time-frame may be extended, as in the changes occurring from early childhood through puberty.

The study of children and infants is ideally suited to this approach, because in this early phase of development a great deal of change occurs in a relatively brief time. In addition, the developmental perspective is valuable for studying the cumulative effects of environmental variables, organismic variables, and the interaction of these two sources of influence.

For example, a developmental psychologist wishes to investigate the role of children's early home environment on their later intellectual performance. The study begins when the subjects are three months of age. Observations are conducted weekly in the children's homes to assess the total amount of stimulation provided by the mother, father, and other family members and the specific types of stimulation involved. Other environmental variables, such as family size, presence of a television, number of toys, and so on, are also noted. When the subjects are twelve months of age, they are given an infant IQ test. They are retested at twenty-four and thirty-six months of age. The results indicate that the quality of the home environment seems to greatly influence intellectual performance. Furthermore, the impact of these early factors is even more evident as the children grow (see Bradley and Caldwell, 1976a, b, for an example of this research).

This study demonstrates how the development approach can be used to trace the suspected influence of a variable over a period of development. In this case, the environment not only had a short-term effect but probably interacted with previous learning experiences or organismic factors to produce even stronger, long-term effects.

At one time the developmental approach was used primarily by psychologists who believed that human behavior was mainly a result of maturational factors. This is no longer the case. The value of this perspective for examining the long-term or interactive influences of environmental effects has become well-established. More recently, the developmental approach has taken a *lifespan* perspective, examining the major changes in human development from birth through old age (see Baltes, Reese, and Nesselroade, 1977).

Cross-Cultural

One disadvantage of investigations conducted in North America is the similar cultural background of the subjects of the research. This is becoming increasingly true as education improves and as the influence of the mass media continues to expand. This similarity is sometimes an advantage in research, because it is one less variable that requires experimental controls. But some experimental questions are difficult to answer when all subjects possess similar experiences or environments.

The best example of this difficulty involves the nature versus nurture issue. For years, psychologists debated and investigated whether human behavior is predominantly a result of inborn (native) variables or external (environmental) variables. We no longer ask this question in such a manner, because there is little doubt that both types of determinants are very important. But a number of specific questions remain that continue to pit internal (for example, genetic) influences against external (for example, learning) influences.

When studying such questions in humans, it is extremely difficult to systematically manipulate genetic variables with sufficient control. Instead, it would seem much easier to focus on the role of the potential environmental factors by varying the backgrounds and experiences of the subjects. But when the available subject population has grown up in the same general culture, this manipulation also proves difficult. Psychologists occasionally have elected to seek comparison subjects from cultures other than our own. The cross-cultural perspective thus permits psychologists to employ different cultural backgrounds as an independent variable. This is one method of partially separating the influence of external factors from biologically based determinants.

For example, a psychologist decides to explore the reports that children in our culture seem to acquire language according to a predictable pattern. That is, their initial speech progresses from certain one- and two-word combinations to more complex grammatical utterances in a manner that can be described by a small number of rules. One theory suggests that these rules are the result of innate processes, which guide the acquisition of language in all humans. An alternative hypothesis is that the rules are more in the psychologist's head than in the child's, and that the common speech patterns are a result of characteristics of the English language or the similarity of language environments.

The psychologist cannot manipulate the suspected internal processes, but he can examine the role of the language background by using a cross-cultural approach. The psychologist collects speech samples from children in the United States, France, Japan, and Kenya. By examining the protocols (samples), the psychologist can determine whether a similar progression of rules seems to apply to the acquisition of each of these languages (see Slobin, 1972; Kagan and Klein, 1972; and Munroe and Munroe, 1975, for more on this approach).

Comparative

In the comparative approach, the psychologist investigates a particular behavior in humans in relation to similar behaviors in other species. Sometimes there is a clear connection between the cross-species behaviors (for example, repro-

FIGURE 3.1
The use of nonhuman species sometimes permits investigations of issues that cannot be studied directly with humans. However, the question of generalizing the findings to our species always remains. (Courtesy University of Wisconsin Primate Laboratory.)

ductive behavior), but at other times the comparison is only assumed or theoretical.

An example of the latter situation involves mother-infant attachment behaviors. Some psychologists suspect that similar mechanisms may guide the attachment process both in humans and in some lower species. The process of *imprinting*, which is apparently responsible for attachment in some bird species, has been one mechanism of interest. Newborn chicks will follow any prominent object (usually the mother) almost immediately after birth. A period of such following seems to result in a unique social attachment to the object, as evidenced by a variety of specific filial behaviors (such as nestling, chirping, and distress calls when the object is removed). Some researchers of human infants have suggested that a similar mechanism may be responsible for infant-mother attachment in our species. But human attachment seems to occur well before the infant is capable of actually pursuing the mother, so some other responses (such as following with the eyes) must be involved. The point of this example is that the comparative approach, based on observations of other species, is sometimes used to generate theoretical hypotheses about human behavior. The hypotheses must, of course, then be confirmed with our own species.

The emphasis of the comparative approach is not always, however, on cross-species similarities. A good deal of research has investigated differences in various aspects of behavior that occur as we proceed up the phylogenetic scale. For example, the speed with which different species can solve a simple discrimination problem, and the nature of the errors produced, may be related to a particular biological characteristic, such as the size of the brain in relation to the rest of the body. Here the emphasis is not focused exclusively on human behavior but is more concerned with animal behavior in general (see Riddell and Corl, 1977).

Comparative research is also useful when specific types of research cannot ethically be conducted with humans. The effects of certain experiences early in life, such as isolation, stress, or disease, are of great interest, but they cannot be directly manipulated in human subjects. Also, the effects of new drugs or radiation treatments must be determined before they can be safely used with humans, but such testing may prove quite dangerous. In these cases, lower animals are frequently used as test subjects. Of course, our ability to confidently draw conclusions from animal simulations remains the subject of some controversy, but there appears to be considerable potential in this approach for better understanding certain areas of human behavior.

Ecological

The fourth approach we shall consider is the ecological approach to investigating human behavior. This approach is very popular in the biological sciences because it concerns the study of the organism in its natural environment. Biologists refer to the relationship of the organism to its environment as its *ecological niche*. The ecological approach is based on the belief that when an animal is removed from its natural surroundings and studied in the laboratory, much information may be lost concerning the actual determinants of its behaviors.

This approach is not new in psychology, but recently its popularity has increased a great deal. This is particularly true in the area of social development. Children's behavior is often studied in relation to aspects of the environment. But, in addition to the physical characteristics of the setting, an important determinant of children's behavior is the *social environment*—that is, other people.

Psychologists have become increasingly interested, for example, in studying *reciprocal relationships* between children or between children and adults. That is, a child's behavior may be determined by aspects of the environment (including other people), but its behavior may also be one determinant of the behavior of other individuals. For example, an infant's smiling behavior is probably determined somewhat by the vocal behavior of the mother, but the smiling may also have some influence on her vocal behavior, thus setting up a circular reaction (Bell, 1971).

Such reciprocal (interdependent) relationships among behaviors can be very complex and difficult to analyze. But this kind of interaction is probably very important for understanding the processes involved in the development of social behaviors. For this reason, ecological psychologists contend that the place to investigate these interactions is in the natural environment. When children are studied in unfamiliar settings by strangers, the typical determinants of their behavior may become impossible to identify.

The principal methods used in this approach have already been mentioned. Typically, nonmanipulative observations are collected in as unobtrusive a manner as possible. Behaviors are observed relative to aspects of the physical and social environment, and the psychologist attempts to identify functional relationships (Gump, 1975; Patterson, 1974).

The major difficulty with this approach is that precise experimental control is often lacking. When using nonmanipulative methods, the experimenter must settle for studying those interactions that occur, rather than simply producing the potential relationships of interest. Some ecological research does involve experimental manipulations that are conducted in the natural setting. But the rigor of the laboratory is almost always somewhat compromised when research is conducted in the field.

Ethological

An approach that is closely related to both the comparative and the ecological approaches is the ethological approach. The principal defining feature of this approach is its interest in the evolutionary origins of behavior. Like the comparative psychologists, ethologists study behaviors in many species; and like the ecological psychologists, they are most concerned with those behaviors occurring in the natural environment.

The ethologists' approach to explaining any behavior has two aspects. The first concerns the present-day determinants, which we discussed in Chapter 1—that is, what are the determinants of the behavior for a particular individual? The second aspect involves the evolutionary influences—that is, why has the behavior evolved in this manner, and how is it adaptive for this particular species? The developmental perspective is often incorporated here as well, since the changes in behavior over time are examined regarding their ultimate survival value.

Human ethologists use methods quite similar to those used by ecological researchers. They emphasize observation in the natural setting, but they may return to the laboratory to pursue an experimental hypothesis generated in the field. Their common characteristic is not one of method, but rather a common theoretical interest in the origins of behavior (see Ainsworth, 1967; Bowlby, 1969, 1973).

These five research approaches should not be considered exhaustive; other approaches used by some child researchers could have been presented. Nor should these approaches be considered completely independent; many areas of behavior can be investigated using a combination of these approaches.

FIGURE 3.2
Cross-cultural studies enable the researcher to examine behavior in children raised in very different environmental circumstances. (Photograph by Emilio A. Mercado.)

For example, developmental issues are often studied cross-culturally or comparatively, and ecological methods are employed by both ethologists and cross-culturalists. What these approaches offer is a way of conceptualizing behavior so that particular issues, such as the nature-nurture controversy, can be addressed more easily.

Experimental Rationale

In this final section, we shall move from discussion of more general methodological approaches to research specifically within the experimental method. The questions we are asking in this section concern the "why" of scientific investigation. Why is a particular experiment carried out? What kinds of information do we anticipate gathering? What sorts of conclusions can we expect to draw from the data? We shall consider three of the most frequent experimental rationale, or reasons for conducting an investigation.

Theory-Testing

Often a researcher plans an experiment specifically to test a theory of behavior. Such research usually involves very well-defined experimental questions, hypotheses, and predictions. It also may focus on a very limited area or involve only a single aspect of the theory.

Experiments sometimes are designed to pit one theory's explanation of a behavior against an alternative theoretical explanation. When the researcher is successful in creating a testable situation where the two theories predict very different outcomes. the experiment is called a *critical test*. The results of the experiment should support one theory and essentially eliminate the other theory. Such critical tests are rare, because the precise conditions necessary to produce the required alternative outcomes are usually very difficult to arrange. For this reason, a number of very different theories may continue to exist, each claiming to explain some aspect of behavior.

Let us consider an unlikely but illustrative experimental situation. A psychologist wishes to explore the finding that young children will imitate aggressive, antisocial behaviors more often than they will imitate cooperative, prosocial behaviors. One theoretical explanation proposes that young children prefer to hurt other children more than to help them. An alternative theory suggests that aggressive behaviors usually involve more physical-motor activity and that young children simply prefer to imitate such higher-level activities. Both of these theories explain the behavior that has been observed. To determine which one is more accurate, the psychologist must design a study in which the two theories predict different outcomes.

In this study, a group of young children observes one model performing a number of aggressive behaviors that involve very little physical activity (for example, hurting another child by booby-trapping his desk or toys). The subjects also observe a second model performing a number of cooperative behaviors that require a good deal of physical motion (for example, helping another child by running around gathering toys for him). The two theories now predict very different outcomes. If the earlier observations of aggression resulted from children's desires to hurt other children, the behaviors of the first model should be imitated. But if the aggression was a result of children's preferences for imitating high-activity behaviors, the second model's cooperative responses should be imitated. It is important to recall, however, that the results of such an experiment can eliminate one theory, but only support (not prove) the other. There may well be other explanations of the imitative behavior that also are consistent with the results of this study, regardless of the outcome (for example, the imitation may be a function of the reactions of the other children).

Again, such critical tests are not very common. More often, a theoretical prediction is simply pitted against the null hypothesis that no significant relationship will be observed between the independent and dependent variables.

If there is any disadvantage to the theory-testing rationale for research, it is that it sometimes blinds the researcher to unexpected but potentially interesting outcomes of the experiment. An unpredicted result may be treated merely as a failure to support the psychologist's theory, and its possible significance may be largely ignored. This is not necessarily the case, however, and the good scientist usually remains open to other interpretations or theoretical explanations when unanticipated findings occur.

Phenomenon Investigation

Not all experimentation is conducted to test a theory. At times, a program of research is carried out for the purpose of investigating a particular phenomenon or a functional relationship of considerable interest.

For example, a very interesting effect is observed when a psychologist rewards children for performing an activity that they were already performing at a high level without reward. The psychologist discovers that when reward is stopped, the children no longer perform the activity at their original high level (Lepper, Greene, and Nisbett, 1973).

In this case, a curious phenomenon has been produced, but little else is known about it. At this point, a large number of questions immediately arise. Under what circumstances does the phenomenon occur? Does it apply equally to males and females? Does it affect people of all ages? Does the type of reward affect results? How long does the effect last? Can it be reversed?

The identification of an unanticipated but interesting effect can thus provide the rationale for an entire series of studies. The early experiments may be designed primarily to "map out" the conditions under which the phenomenon occurs. Gradually, as theoretical explanations are proposed, more specific hypothesis-testing may begin.

Exploration

Research is not always designed to test a specific theory or even to investigate a particular functional relationship. Sometimes psychologists conduct investigations simply to explore potential relations between independent and dependent variables. Such exploratory research probably is not as common as the two forms just described, but it has a definite place in psychological research.

The fact that research is exploratory does not mean, however, that it is a random process. A psychologist setting out to probe an area usually has some interest in the effects of a particular independent variable or is concerned with the various influences on a specific behavior.

For example, a psychologist may be interested in the behavioral effects on the newborn of a new drug given to mothers during childbirth. A wide range of behaviors in the newborns (such as sleeping patterns, feeding, pain sensitivity) may be compared with the same behaviors in a group of control subjects. The purpose of these studies is to identify relationships between this independent variable (drug) and any behavior in the newborns—even if no specific hypotheses or predictions have been proposed. As a second example, a researcher may be interested in determining some of the variables affecting children's friendship preferences. The psychologist might examine such factors as length of acquaintance, physical similarities, and mutual interests, with the intention of locating one or more important sources of influence. Here a dependent variable (friendship preference) provides the basis for the series of exploratory studies.

The typical progression of research in an area is perhaps more frequently the reverse of what we have presented. Exploratory research initially may lead to the discovery of an interesting phenomenon. Investigations of the phenomenon result in a number of possible theoretical explanations, which leads to a series of theory-testing experiments. This progression is somewhat simplistic, but it illustrates the different purposes served by these three forms of experimentation.

Conclusion

It should now be obvious that psychological research can take many forms. A number of the less-popular research methods were not discussed in this chapter, yet a variety of dimensions, perspectives, and rationale were presented. Perhaps this diversity is the reason that so much disagreement and controversy exists on some issues, but it is also one of psychology's greatest strengths. With a subject as complex as human behavior, the wide range of questions and investigatory approaches that psychologists have used seems to offer the best means to understanding human behavior.

Part I has been concerned with fundamentals and generalities. In Part II we shall become somewhat more specific as we examine the three principal types of research designs. These chapters build on what already has been presented, however, and it may be useful to return to the first chapters as fundamental concepts begin to reappear.

References

Ainsworth, M. D. S. *Infancy in Uganda: Infant care and growth of attachment.* Baltimore: Johns Hopkins University Press, 1967.

Baltes, P. B., Reese, H. W., and Nesselroade, J. R. *Life-span developmental psychology: Introduction to research methods.* Monterey, Calif.: Brooks/Cole, 1977.

Bell, R. Q. Stimulus control of parent or caretaker behavior by offspring. *Developmental Psychology,* 1971, **4,** 63–72.

Bowlby, J. Attachment. In *Attachment and loss* (Vol. 1). New York: Basic Books, 1969.

Bowlby, J. Separation: Anxiety and anger. In *Attachment and loss* (Vol. 2). New York: Basic Books, 1973.

Bradley, R., and Caldwell, B. Early home environments and changes in mental test performance in children from 6 to 36 months. *Developmental Psychology,* 1976, **12,** 93–94. (a)

Bradley, R., and Caldwell, B. The relation of infants' home environments to mental test performance at 54 months: a follow-up study. *Child Development,* 1976, **47,** 1172–1174. (b)

Gump, P. V. Ecological psychology and children. In E. M. Hetherington (ed.), *Review of child development research* (Vol. 5). Chicago: University of Chicago Press, 1975.

Kagan, J., and Klein, R. E. Cross-cultural perspectives on early development. In E. M. Hetherington and R. D. Parke (eds.), *Contemporary readings in child psychology.* New York: McGraw-Hill, 1977.

Lepper, M. R., Greene, D., and Nisbett, R. E. Undermining children's intrinsic interest with extrinsic reward: A test of the "overjustification" hypothesis. *Journal of Personality and Social Psychology,* 1973, **28,** 129–137.

Munroe, R. L., and Munroe, R. H. *Cross-cultural human development.* Monterey, Calif.: Brooks/Cole, 1965.

Patterson, G. R. A basis for identifying stimuli which control behaviors in natural settings. *Child Development,* 1974, **45,** 900–911.

Reese, H. W., and Lipsitt, L. P. *Experimental child psychology.* New York: Academic Press, 1970, Chapter 1.

Riddell, W. I., and Corl, K. G. Comparative investigation of the relationship between cerebral indices and learning abilities. *Brain, Behavior and Evolution,* 1977, **14,** 385–398.

Slobin, D. I. They learn the same way all around the world. *Psychology Today,* July, 1972.

II

Basic
Research
Designs

4 Longitudinal Research

One important approach to the study of child development is longitudinal research. This approach is actually not so much a research design as it is a research perspective. For example, we shall see that this type of study can involve either experimental-manipulative methods (which we discussed previously) or correlational-observational methods (which we shall consider shortly), although the latter are much more common. In fact, longitudinal research is frequently presented simply as one form of the more general correlational research method. Our decision to devote a separate chapter to this approach, however, is based upon its relative popularity among child researchers, its usefulness in addressing important issues in human development, and its historical significance. Because so much of the correlational research conducted by child psychologists involves the longitudinal approach, we shall include our discussion of correlational methodology as part of this chapter.

Longitudinal research is one of the oldest methods of child study. The earliest attempts to observe and record the behavior and development of children typically took the form of a diary or daily account of the child's progress over the first years of life. These observations, reported as early as the eighteenth century, were frequently made on the investigator's own children and have become known as *baby biographies*. The focus of these studies was almost always on changes in the physical aspects of growth and their relationship to the child's age. Much of this research involved observational methods, which will be discussed in Chapter 10.

Rationale

The longitudinal design is often based on the developmental perspective. The information of greatest interest typically is the changes that occur in various aspects of behavior over an extended period of time. As with most developmental research, the focus was originally on the influence of innate, biological variables. But the role of environmental and experiential factors has also become the subject of longitudinal studies in recent years.

The procedures usually involve selecting a large sample of young subjects and initially testing them on a battery of assessment instruments or other dependent measures. The number of different dependent variables in the study is often relatively large, and the researcher attempts to obtain as much information as possible from the single investigation. The subsequent assessments of the dependent variables typically occur at regular intervals (such as every month or semiannually) and continue for a period of years.

By studying the same children over a period of time, longitudinal investigations permit a detailed examination of changes in the behavior of individual subjects. More importantly, this intensive approach can be very useful for identifying the most important variables responsible for producing these changes.

For example, the role of early experiences on later behavior has traditionally been an important issue for developmental psychologists. Such variables as maternal deprivation, stress, or restricted practice have been the subject of a good deal of human and comparative research. Using the longitudinal approach, the researcher can note the occurrence of these early environmental events and examine their relationship to behavior later in the organism's life (see Harlow and Suomi, 1970).

Experimental Studies

Longitudinal investigations occasionally involve the experimental method. An independent variable is systematically manipulated over a period of time, and potential changes in a target behavior are continually observed. One of the classic examples of this type of approach involved the method of the *co-twin control* (Gesell and Thompson, 1929; McGraw, 1935). Researchers in the 1920s and 1930s were interested in the possible effects of practice or training on the development of children's motor skills. At that time, many psychologists believed that the emergence of motor behaviors was a result of simple maturation or inborn genetic influences. Training and practice were believed to play a minimal role at best, and extra training was not predicted to accelerate the development of the child's motor skills.

To test these theoretical ideas, pairs of identical twins were used as subjects, because their genetic makeup was also identical. At several weeks of age, a training program was begun for the experimental twin. This may have included daily practice in crawling, standing, stair-climbing, or other motor behaviors. The control twin received no extra practice. Periodically, the two were tested on various motor behaviors to observe the effects of the extra practice. This type of study sometimes continued until the subjects were eight or nine years old.

In this case, the longitudinal approach involved nothing more than a simple experiment, which was conducted over a long period of time. Not all longitudinal research, however, is experimental in nature.

Correlational Studies

The more common longitudinal study does not involve separate groups of subjects receiving separate experiences, but treats all individuals in the same manner. Often such research is more descriptive in character, with no manipulation or intervention by the researcher. Rather, the emphasis is on identifying variables occurring early in the period of observation and *correlating* them with behaviors occurring at some later time. Before discussing this method, let us briefly consider the nature of correlational research as compared with the experimental method.

A *correlation* is a statistical term meaning that two variables change or vary together in a predictable way. But unlike a functional relationship, it does not necessarily imply that changes in one variable cause the changes in the other variable. It simply describes the patterns of variation.

A *positive correlation* means that the two variables change in the same direction—that is, as one increases, the other increases, or as one decreases, the other decreases. A *negative correlation* means that the two vary in opposite directions—for example, as one goes up, the other goes down. Such mutual variation is rarely perfect, however, and the variables may only approximately fit these patterns. We can, therefore, also express the strength of the relationship.

A perfectly positive correlation is expressed as +1.00. This number gradually decreases to 0.00 as the relationship between the two variables decreases. A perfectly negative correlation is expressed as −1.00, and the number gradually increases to 0.00 as the relationship decreases. So, a correlation of +0.21 indicates a weakly positive relationship between two variables, and a correlation of −0.82 indicates a strongly negative correlation (see Figure 4.1).

For example, there is a strong positive correlation between children's heights and weights. As we examine children of increasing height, we observe that their average weight also increases. There obviously are some exceptions to this relationship, so the positive correlation is not perfect (+1.00). A negative correlation is illustrated by the relationship between a child's age and the number of hours each day spent with the mother. The number of these hours tends to decrease as the child grows older.

Notice that in neither case have we suggested a *causal* relationship. That is, increasing height does not necessarily cause increasing weight, nor vice versa; being away from mother does not cause an increase in age, nor does increasing age automatically result in maternal separation. These correla-

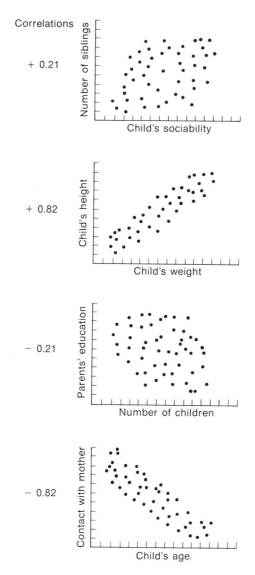

FIGURE 4.1
Scatter-diagram illustrating hypothetical correlations between two variables. The value of one variable is plotted on the vertical axis, and the value of the second variable is plotted on the horizontal axis. The top graphs depict positive correlations, where increases in one variable generally correspond to increases in the second variable. The lower graphs depict negative correlations, where higher values of one variable are related to lower values of the other variable.

tions simply represent patterns of variation; the actual determinants are not specified. It is *possible* that changes in one of the variables may cause the changes in the other, but a correlation statistic does not provide us with this information. Nor does it permit us to reject other explanations; for example, changes in the two variables may be a result of some unidentified third variable. Only through experimentation can such functional relationships be determined. Correlational findings are often useful, however, for suggesting potential relationships which then can be investigated using experimental methods. This is the strategy of the longitudinal-correlational approach.

For example, a researcher may be interested in investigating a particular form of environmental stimulation (viewing an educational television program such as *Sesame Street*) and the effects of this stimulation on a subsequent behavior (reading ability in elementary school). A longitudinal-correlational approach to this investigation might begin by noting the average number of hours a large group of preschool children spends each week watching such programming. A distribution of scores (hours) would probably result, with some children spending a great many hours in this activity, some spending only a few, and the majority falling somewhere in between. The investigator would then follow the reading progress of these subjects for the next five or six years, perhaps assessing their reading levels each spring. Again, a distribution of reading abilities would be expected. Note that no manipulation of variables has taken place—only observation of the events and behaviors in the natural setting.

After the data on the two variables had been collected, the investigator would use correlational statistical methods to examine the relationship between the two distributions of scores. If they were very similar—that is, if the children who watched the most educational television had the highest reading scores and the ones who watched the least had the lowest scores—a positive correlation between these two variables would be evident. These results would *indicate* that the amount of educational television viewing and subsequent reading ability vary in the same way, and they might be taken to *suggest* that differences in the first variable cause differences in the second. But that suggestion would then require experimental investigation, because a number of alternative interpretations of these results are possible. For example, children who read more may find educational television easier to understand, and thus they may prefer it more than nonreaders do. Or the relationship between the two variables may be caused by a third influence (e.g., encouragement from parents to participate in these two activities). *The causal relationship cannot be identified using only correlational methods.*

By this point, it may be obvious how the hypothesis suggested by these data (educational television improves reading) could be investigated experimentally. A representative group of children might systematically be exposed to educational television, while a control group receives no contact with these programs. At the end of the study, a comparison of reading abilities (dependent variables) would indicate any positive effects of the television viewing (manipulated variable). Although this design appears simple enough, you may detect a number of practical and ethical problems with such a study. We shall discuss some of these issues in Chapter 11.

The major differences among true-experimental, quasi-experimental, and correlational studies lies in our ability to interpret the results of the investigation with confidence. True experiments permit us to reject most potential, alternative explanations of the findings and to accept the experimental hypothesis with reasonable confidence. Quasi-experiments and correlational studies in particular, may produce data that are consistent with our predictions but that may be open to other explanations.

It may be instructive to consider two other possible results of our hypothetical investigation. The data might have revealed a negative correlation between the two variables. For instance, if watching television interfered with the time the children might otherwise have spent reading, the opposite effect might have been demonstrated—children who spent the most time watching television (even educational programs) would have produced the lowest reading scores. Another possible result might have been that the two variables were unrelated—that is, differences in one variable were not systematically related to differences in the other at all. In this case, the correlation between educational television viewing and reading ability would be close to 0.00.

Another way to think about correlational data is in terms of their *predictability*. If knowing the value of one variable allows us to predict the value of the second variable with a high degree of accuracy, then the correlation between them is high (positive or negative). If knowing the value of one variable provides virtually no information about the possible value of the other, the correlation between them is close to 0.00.

A major advantage of the longitudinal-correlational design is that it permits the researcher to investigate relationships between a large number of independent and dependent variables simultaneously. The psychologist can observe a dozen different environmental or organismic variables at some point early in the investigation and assess a dozen different dependent measures later in the study. Using the appropriate statistical methods, the researcher can determine which variables are correlated and whether the relationship is positive or negative. The more interesting findings can then be pursued experimentally to try to identify causal relationships between them. If the researcher had begun instead with an experimental approach, the effort required to manipulate systematically all twelve independent variables, including appropriate control procedures, would have been considerably greater. Longitudinal-correlational studies thus do not in themselves answer causal questions, but they help us to determine which questions are most useful to continue to ask.

Disadvantages

The longitudinal approach unfortunately has a number of undesirable characteristics that present problems for the psychologist. Some of these are simply troublesome practical difficulties; others are more technical. But unless all of them are dealt with adequately, a great deal of time and effort may be wasted collecting data that prove to be of little value.

Sample Characteristics

Several common problems concern the subjects of longitudinal investigations. Representative sampling often poses a major difficulty, because the commitment required from the subjects is unusually demanding. Typically, the parents of the children in the sample must agree to participate in the study for the entire course of the research. This involves maintaining constant contact with the research team, even if the family moves, and permitting periodic assessment of the children by the investigators. At times, the parents may also be required to supply observations or other data at regular intervals throughout the study.

When such research is planned over a five- or ten-year period, it is not surprising that obtaining a group of subjects may not be an easy task. But the important point is that those parents who are willing to commit this amount of effort to the research may not be representative of the larger population. Perhaps they are more concerned, better educated, more curious, or less suspicious. The potential difficulty, then, is one of starting the research with a biased sample of parents and children.

Even if the investigator is successful in initially selecting a representative group, a related potential problem involves the nature of *subject attrition*. That is, some subjects invariably will drop out or be lost from the research for various reasons. Again, this raises the possibility of sample bias. Perhaps the subjects who remain in the study are more cooperative, more persistent, less assertive, or more stable. In this way, an originally representative sample may become biased as subjects drop out in a *nonrandom* fashion. And, of course, if too many subjects are lost, the sample size may become too small to allow the psychologist to draw any legitimate conclusions from the results.

Variable Selection

Another type of difficulty concerns the decision as to which variables to include in the investigation. We mentioned that it is much easier to study a large number of variables when the research is correlational in nature, but the number nevertheless must be reasonable.

One of the problems here is that the questions asked at the beginning of the study are often difficult to change once the research has begun. If the psychologist wishes to consider additional variables and questions, perhaps as a result of findings from other research during this period, it may be impossible to include these measures. The research thus may have to be completed with many potentially answerable questions unaddressed. An even greater concern is that some of the initial measures may later be demonstrated to be inaccurate, biased, or not completely valid. In this case, data collected over many years may suddenly be virtually useless.

Sometimes the instruments used to assess dependent measures change during the period of observation. IQ tests, for example, are periodically updated and restandardized. If the psychologist does not use the newer tests as they are developed, there is the risk that the older tests are no longer valid indicators of the behavior. But if the newer tests are used, there may be some difficulty in comparing scores on these tests with scores on the older tests.

The general problem here is that time and research do not stand still while longitudinal investigations are being conducted. It should not be surprising, then, that some aspects of the research may well be out of date even before the study is completed.

Repeated Testing

A third problem that sometimes arises is the repeated administration of measures to assess the behaviors of interest. We saw in Chapter 2 that children at times become "test-wise" and improve their scores on tests simply as a function of repeated practice. Longitudinal studies almost always require assessment of the dependent measure at regular intervals. The likelihood of this type of problem thus depends primarily on the frequency with which the tests are administered.

Parents also may become aware of the nature of the tests or observations used in the research. Often without intending to they may begin to exert some effect on those aspects of the child's behavior that are under study. For example, if the investigators frequently assess the child's language skills, the parents may realize that this is an important area of interest. Their reactions to the child's ungrammatical statements, or even the language they use themselves, may reflect their knowledge of the research and unintentionally (or even deliberately) affect the study's findings.

Historical Events

One of the most difficult problems in longitudinal research, which we discussed briefly in Chapter 2, involves historical circumstances and events. The particular time-frame during which any longitudinal study takes place possesses a variety of unique historical characteristics as compared with any other period of years. Political events, current social values, economic conditions, and the like all may produce an atmosphere very different from the same time-span studied at an earlier or later date.

For example, consider an investigation attempting to examine the relationship between early parental discipline techniques and the later social behavior of the child. Very different effects might result from strict parental control, for instance, if it occurs in the context of a very permissive social climate rather than during an era of rigid moral values. More specific historical events, such as a presidential assassination or a severe flood, may also have disruptive and perhaps long-term effects on various social relationships under study.

Providing the appropriate control procedures for these factors is not very easy for the psychologist. Theoretically, the best solution would be to replicate the study with another group of subjects. By repeating the study during a different time-period, the potential effects of the background historical conditions can be observed. Any other type of control procedure would fall somewhat short of providing the information

TABLE 4.1
Problems of Longitudinal Research

Problems	Causes
Biased sample	Initial selection difficulties; nonrandom attrition
Obsolete data	Changing research questions; updated instruments
Biased data	Repeated testing; parental expectations; historical events
Uncompleted project	High cost; extended time-period; personnel changes

necessary to rule out alternative explanations of the data. But replicating a longitudinal study is not a very attractive prospect, and in fact it rarely occurs.

Additional Problems

A number of more practical problems also frequently arise in longitudinal research. The most obvious difficulty is the amount of time required to answer the theoretical questions of interest. If the results concern practical issues, or even if they are relevant to a theory that a psychologist is developing, the need to wait years for the missing evidence may be too high a price to pay for selecting this type of research design.

Related to the time factor are a number of other problems, such as the high cost of long-term projects and the large amounts of data that must continually be analyzed. Finally, unexpected loss of research personnel or even the principal investigator is quite possible and can interfere with the efficient progress of the investigation. See Table 4.1 for a summary of the main problems and their causes in longitudinal research.

Alternatives

The many problems associated with the longitudinal design have led psychologists to seek alternative methods of developmental research without sacrificing the advantages of the longitudinal method. Two very different approaches have been attempted.

Combined Longitudinal/Cross-Sectional Design

One alternative has been to combine the longitudinal design with the cross-sectional design in an attempt to retain the best features of both. Cross-sectional studies examine developmental questions by comparing groups of subjects at different age levels rather than following the same individuals for many years. This method is much faster than the long-term approach, but it is subject to some of the problems we discussed earlier, such as generational effects. More importantly, it does not permit close-up analysis of changes in individual subjects, which is the primary advantage of the longitudinal method.

In a *combined longitudinal/cross-sectional design*, several groups of subjects at different ages are studied over a period of years. For example, we might begin with groups at ages one, four, seven, and ten. Our initial assessment of the dependent measures would demonstrate any developmental differences in performance over these four age-levels. If we then continued to study these subjects for a three-year period, our samples would be four, seven, ten, and thirteen years of age. Now we would have three years of data on each individual, permitting an in-depth examination of the determinants of the behavior of interest. We would also have comparison data at three of the age-levels. These data would serve both as replications of the original findings, and as controls against generational effects. In many ways, this design offers an excellent tool for addressing a wide range of developmental questions.

Retrospective Design

A second alternative to the longitudinal method is the *retrospective* approach. Psychologists attempting to link an individual's current behavior with events early in his or her life will sometimes have the subject describe the circumstances occurring during childhood. Questionnaires or structured interviews are often used to uncover various aspects of the subject's past. The questions might cover such topics as specific environmental characteristics (size of home, number in family, typical diet), social variables (parental disciplinary practices, friendships, school experiences), and emotions or attitudes possessed at the time. Correlations between earlier events and current behavior are examined to try to identify possible cause-and-effect relationships. Of course, these hypothetical relationships never can be tested directly with these subjects, but they can serve as the basis for experimental research with other individuals.

The principal difficulty with the retrospective approach involves the reliability and validity of the reports. It is well-known, both casually and experimentally, that many variables affect accuracy of memory. Sometimes our recollections are distorted by events that occurred during the intervening years or events that are occurring at the moment. At times we may seem to recall things because we have heard about them from others. When in doubt, the subject may be inclined to produce the *socially desirable* response; that is, the subject may tell the psychologist the information that seems to be expected. Finally, an important determinant of an individual's behavior may not be revealed if the questionnaire is not sufficiently broad and if the subject is not aware of its importance. Thus, retrospective accounts can provide intriguing and perhaps researchable possibilities, but they offer very little to a scientific analysis on their own.

Conclusion

The longitudinal research design offers the psychologist a potentially valuable way to focus on changes in behavior and to identify the determinants of such change. In addition, it permits the study of the long-term, cumulative effects of these variables and their interaction with one another.

The many difficulties inherent in this approach, however, have led many psychologists to prefer more short-term, experimental methods of research. Psychology is a relatively young science, and progress is being made very rapidly. There is some impatience in pursuing long-term investigations when so much can be learned in short-term studies. The combined longitudinal/cross-sectional approach, however, seems to be increasing in popularity and may provide an excellent method for dealing with a number of developmental issues.

References

Gesell, A., and Thompson, H. Learning and growing in identical twins: An experimental study by the method of co-twin control. *Genetic Psychology Monographs*, 1929, **6**, 1–24.

Harlow, H. F., and Suomi, S. J. Nature of love—simplified. *American Psychologist*, 1970, **25**, 161–168.

McGraw, M. B. *Growth: A study of Johnny and Jimmy.* New York: Appleton-Century-Crofts, 1935.

5 Experimental Research

In this chapter we shall consider some of the basic research designs used in the experimental study of children's behavior. In contrast to the longitudinal approach, most experimental research is relatively short-term in nature (the longitudinal experimental design is, of course, an exception). The shorter time-frame is possible because experimental studies usually involve comparisons of separate groups of subjects rather than a single sample studied over time. Some of the desirable features of long-term methods are certainly lost with this approach, but other advantages have made experimental methods currently far more popular among child psychologists.

The experimental designs outlined in this chapter involve a number of statistical concepts and issues. We shall describe and illustrate these concepts at only a very general level. The mathematical detail necessary to learn to conduct actual statistical analyses of experimental data goes beyond the purpose of this text. This type of information can be obtained in a textbook on elementary statistical methods, and the interested student is encouraged to pursue such reading. Our purpose is to introduce the descriptions and rationale of the various experimental designs in such a way that the student encountering them for the first time will not be overwhelmed by numbers, notations, and equations. These, too, are important and, of course, should eventually be mastered as well.

A Typical Research Study

Let us consider a very simple (and hypothetical) experiment. A psychologist wishes to study performance on a visual-spatial task as a function of the size of the test stimuli. The investigator has reason to believe that subjects will perform better on such a task when very large stimuli are employed as compared with smaller stimuli. Only two groups of subjects will be used in this experiment—a group tested with large stimuli compared with a group tested with small stimuli.

This study represents one of the simplest experimental designs. There is only one independent variable (size of stimuli), and it can assume only two different values (small, large) along a dimension. In experimental research, the dimension is referred to as a *factor*, and each value along that factor is called a *level*. Our example, then, would be described as a single-factor design with two levels of the independent variable. We shall now consider each step in the experimental process and examine some of the experimental and practical problems that the researcher must address.

Sample Selection

We must begin by selecting samples of subjects. In Chapter 2 we discussed why it is necessary for the composition of the groups to be the same at the outset. There are two ways to achieve such equivalence.

The first of these is *matching*. We can select our two samples so that the subjects are equal or matched on a number of variables. For instance, we might match the ages of the subjects, their educational levels, their socioeconomic backgrounds, and so on. Matching can mean either using only one level of each variable (for example, only twelve-year-olds in each group), or matching the proportions of subjects at each level (for example, 15 percent ten-year-olds, 25 percent eleven-year-olds, 60 percent twelve-year-olds). Each time another variable is matched for our samples, it is eliminated as a possible alternative explanation in the study—that is, it could not account for any differences later observed between groups. One of the disadvantages of the matching procedure, however, is that the more variables on which subjects are matched, the larger must be the population from which the subjects are sampled. If we wanted to match our subjects on age, we might select only from the twelve-year-olds in the population. But if we also wanted to match on education, we might select only from those subjects who were twelve-years-old *and* in the fourth grade. As the number of matched variables increases, the number of available subjects possessing the proper combination of characteristics (levels) quickly decreases. It is, of course, impossible to match our two samples on every conceivable variable. And some variables, such as foot size or middle initial, would hardly be expected to present competing explanations to any differences in performance that might occur. When variables are matched, then, it is only done for those that would most likely offer reasonable alternative interpretations of the data if they varied systematically with the independent variable under study.

To deal with the remaining unmatched variables, we must rely on a second procedure for assigning subjects—*randomization*. You will recall from Chapter 2 that many subject characteristics are distributed unsystematically throughout the population—that is, each individual possesses a different combination of characteristics. If two samples of subjects are selected randomly from such a population, it would be very unlikely that they would vary systematically on any one variable. For example, there would be a very small chance of unintentionally selecting groups where one contained only blue-eyed subjects and the other only brown-eyed subjects. And, of course, the larger the samples, the less likely are such unusual occurrences.

Using these two procedures, we can ensure that the subjects in the two groups do not vary systematically on any characteristic before the experimental treatment is administered. Matching guarantees that this will not happen by specifically dividing subjects possessing the same levels of a variable between the two groups. Randomization, in contrast, does not specifically assign subjects according to their characteristics, but simply assigns them randomly and *assumes* that no systematic variation has occurred. The larger the number of subjects in each sample, the more reasonable is this assumption.

We can now consider how we might actually select the subjects for our hypothetical experiment. We would begin by selecting the initial population, such as the local elementary school, from which to draw our samples. Because age and sex may be variables that are very much related to performance on our dependent measure, we decide to match the two groups on these characteristics. In this case we narrow our potential population to all the ten-year-olds in the school. To select our actual samples, we obtain a list of the names of all the ten-year-old males and females in the school and place the names in separate hats. The first eight male and eight female names we draw from the hats become one group, and the next eight of each sex become the second group. We assume that these samples are representative of the populations under study; we know that they do not differ systematically in age or sex; and we rely on randomization to assure that they do not vary systematically on any other variable. We are now prepared to conduct the experiment.

Data Collection

Each different experiment will have its own unique combination of characteristics that must be dealt with or controlled. Here we shall consider the common situation where the experiment is conducted in the school building during the normal class day.

The fundamental rule of conducting an experiment is that each subject must be studied under as standard a set of conditions as possible. Again, this is necessary to ensure that the only differences among subjects are those we impose by the experimental manipulation. This standardization is achieved in a variety of ways.

Each child usually is taken from the classroom to a separate room where the task is performed. The use of a single experimental room standardizes the physical aspects of the situation, such as the size of the room, lighting, temperature, distractions, and so on. In some research, the time of day that the subjects are studied might be important; this applies to any task where fatigue or alertness may play an important role. Some researchers also prefer not to collect data just before or after school vacations, because they feel that these are not typical times. Most often, the same experimenter collects all the data, unless some characteristic of the experimenter (such as gender or race) happens to be one of the independent variables under study.

Although the experimenter should be well-versed in the procedures, there may be some tendency for practice to make the procedures slightly smoother, faster, or different in some other way. For this reason, and others, the order in which subjects are studied should be distributed across experimental groups, so that one entire group is not studied, for example, during the first days of the experiment and another group studied during the final days. Whenever possible, it is a good idea for the experimenter not to be familiar with the actual hypotheses under study. This is a caution against possible *experimenter bias*—that is, unintentional and often subtle changes in the experimenter's behavior with certain subjects which increase the chances of finding the predicted results. When it is impossible to keep the experimenter unaware of the hypotheses, it may be possible at least to conceal the experimental group to which each subject belongs.

A very important part of the experimental procedures are the instructions to the subject. It is often crucial that all subjects (in a particular experimental group, perhaps) receive precisely the same instructions delivered in the same manner. This is, in fact, one place where experimenter bias is most likely to occur. One solution is to have the experimenter simply read the instructions; an even better method is to play them for the

subject on a tape recorder. The primary function of the instructions is to make the task perfectly clear. In addition, the instructions sometimes involve a motivational component, such
as a prize or more abstract reward (for example, praise) for
doing well on the task. This type of incentive is used to guarantee at least some minimum level of motivation and interest by
all subjects.

In our example, the experiment involves an embedded-
figures task. Each subject is brought to the experimental room,
seated at a table, and instructed how to perform the task. A
series of twenty-five cards are presented one at a time, each
containing an embedded-figures problem. The problems consist of a complex geometrical figure in which a simple geometrical shape is hidden. The subject is shown a sample of the
simple figure and instructed to try to locate it in each complex
design as quickly as possible. The dependent measure in our
study is the number of problems the subject solves in less than
fifteen seconds each. Each subject thus can receive a score of 0
to 25.

Data Analysis and Interpretation

After all the data have been collected, they must be
analyzed to determine their meaning. Suppose the scores we
obtained in our experiment are those presented in Table 5.1a.
From these data, what could we conclude about our hypothesis
that subjects perform better with large stimuli than small
stimuli on the embedded-figures task? To begin, the two sets of
results are difficult to compare in terms of the total collections
of *raw scores*, so we want to summarize the group data in some
way. The most useful *summary statistic* that we can use to
describe the data is the *mean*, or average score for each group.
In Table 5.1b, we can see that the mean score for large stimuli
is over four points greater than the mean score for small
stimuli. This difference would suggest support for our hypothesis. But before we can accept the hypothesis, we must determine that the likelihood of obtaining a difference of this size by
chance variability alone is less than five percent. To calculate

TABLE 5.1
Performance on Embedded-Figures Task (Group 1)

	Large Stimuli	Small Stimuli
	18	11
	16	18
	21	10
	17	12
	13	12
(a)	20	13
Raw Scores	15	20
	21	14
	14	13
	22	9
	8	10
	19	15
	10	7
	23	8
	13	11
	17	14
(b) Mean (Average) Scores	16.68	12.31
(c) Standard Deviations	4.19	3.33
(d) t Values	$t = 3.16$ ($t = 2.13$ or greater is necessary to reject null hypothesis)	

this probability, a second summary statistic is needed. We must determine how much *variability* exists within each group of scores—that is, how far around the mean score are the other scores distributed? One measure of the variability of a set of scores is the *standard deviation*. This statistic indicates the degree to which the scores are spread out within the group rather than tightly clustered about the mean. The standard deviations for our two groups are presented in Table 5.1c.

Using these two summary statistics, we can now apply inferential statistical methods to determine whether the mean differences are greater than would be expected by chance, given the amount of variability that exists in each group. One popular test used to analyze such results is the *t test*. In very general terms, the *t test* is a ratio of the differences between the means of the samples compared with a measure of the variability in the two samples. This ratio can be expressed as:

$$t = \frac{\text{Difference between means}}{\text{Variability within groups}}$$

As the difference between group means grows larger, the value of t increases; as the variability within groups increases, the value of t decreases. Larger values of t, therefore, increase our confidence that the differences observed between the two experimental groups are not simply a result of chance. That is, larger values of t are necessary to indicate a functional relationship between our independent and dependent variables.

Exactly how large must the value of t be before we can decide that our results are less than the five percent level of probability? This value is determined by the number of subjects in each group—as the sample sizes grow larger, the necessary value of t gets smaller. For example, in our experiment with sixteen subjects per group, the value of t necessary to accept the experimental hypothesis is 2.13. This value is obtained from a table of t-scores included in most standard statistics texts. We can see that the actual value of t in the data (t = 3.16) is greater than 2.13 (Table 5.1d); therefore, we can conclude that the findings support our prediction that performance is better with large stimuli. In such a case, we say that the performance with the two sets of stimuli was *significantly different*, meaning statistically different beyond the five percent chance probability level.

Now let us compare these data with the results presented in Table 5.2. Here we have repeated the study and obtained another set of scores (Table 5.2a). Note that the difference between the mean scores for each group is slightly greater than in our first example (Table 5.2b). This larger difference suggests that these results display even greater support for the experimental hypothesis. But these data differ from the first data in variability as well. The larger standard deviations indicate that the scores of both groups display greater variability

TABLE 5.2
Performance on Embedded-Figures Task (Group 2)

	Large Stimuli	Small Stimuli
	24	8
	16	21
	24	8
	12	18
	10	16
(a)	23	5
Raw Scores	8	21
	24	9
	13	17
	23	7
	6	8
	23	17
	7	6
	25	9
	12	9
	23	17
(b) Mean (Average) Scores	17.06	12.25
(c) Standard Deviations	6.95	5.43
(d) t Values	$t = 2.11$ ($t = 2.13$ or greater is necessary to reject null hypothesis)	

than in the first study (Table 5.1c.) When these results are subjected to a t-test, the value of the ratio is now considerably lower (Table 5.1d). In fact, it is slightly too low to conclude that the differences are not simply a result of chance variability. We therefore cannot reject the null hypothesis that no differences exist between the performance of the two groups on our dependent measure. In this case, the differences would be described as statistically *nonsignificant*.

We have not included the mathematical equations necessary actually to conduct these analyses, but the general approach to data analysis and interpretation should be relatively clear. In particular, we must be as concerned about differences in scores that occur within groups as we are with the differences observed between groups. This will continue to be true as we proceed to more complex designs.

Single-Factor Design

The two-group example in the last section is the simplest type of single-factor experimental design. Studies involving three, four, or more levels of the independent variable are fairly common.

Consider a study where the investigator is interested in whether different amounts of exposure to a peer-model playing with a toy influence the amount of time that observing children spend playing with the toy if given an opportunity (that is, amount of imitation). Four levels of the independent variable are included—one, five, fifteen, or thirty minutes of exposure to the model. Ten subjects are randomly assigned to each exposure condition. The dependent measure is the number of minutes each subject later spends playing with the toy. The scores of this hypothetical experiment are presented in Table 5.3.

TABLE 5.3
Amount of Imitation (Group 1)

| | Exposure (Minutes) | | | |
	1	5	15	30
	6	8	10	17
	4	6	13	19
	5	5	15	18
	6	7	10	21
Raw Scores	3	8	11	23
	5	3	12	20
	4	2	8	19
	4	6	11	18
	2	4	9	18
	1	5	12	22
Mean Scores	4.0	5.4	11.1	19.5

$F = 135.31$ ($F = 2.89$ or greater is necessary to reject null hypothesis)

Again we can calculate important summary statistics, such as the mean score for each group and their standard deviations. To analyze the results of more than two groups, a test known as the *F test* or *analysis of variance* is frequently used. This test is conceptually similar to the *t test;* it is the ratio of the variability between group scores compared with the variability within group scores. This ratio would be expressed as:

$$F = \frac{\text{Variability between groups}}{\text{Variability within groups}}$$

As the difference between group scores grows larger, or as the scores within groups become more compact (less variable), the value of F increases. Larger values of F lead to greater likelihood of rejecting the null hypothesis that there are no real differences between the groups.

In this case, an F value of 2.89 is necessary to reject the null hypothesis. The analysis conducted on the investigator's data yielded an F of 135.31, which obviously indicates statistically significant differences among the groups. Further analyses would be necessary to determine precisely where the differences lay; but at least the psychologist can be sure at this point that the results represent more than random variability within the groups. That is, some sort of functional relationship exists between the amount of exposure children have to a peer-model and the amount of time they spend engaging in similar behavior.

A special case of the single-factor design is the *repeated measures design*. Here the various sets of scores do not represent different groups of subjects but are different scores by the same subjects. For example, in the last study the researcher might have selected ten subjects and studied them under each of the four exposure conditions. Following each exposure to the peer-model, the subject would once again have been given an opportunity to play with the toy. In this case, the different levels of the independent variable are examined *within subjects* rather than *between subjects*. Such studies require that we control for a number of additional factors, particularly the order in which the different conditions are presented. But the variability within groups is often less with this procedure, making the design somewhat more sensitive to the effects of the independent manipulation. A modified version of the F test can also be used to analyze results from this design (when only two levels are involved, a modified t test can be used).

Multiple-Factor Designs

The experimental designs we have considered thus far permit us to investigate only one independent variable at a time. It would be much more efficient if several independent manipulations could occur within the same set of experimental procedures. The multiple-factor design allows for just such a tactic.

Two-Factor Design

Let us consider the previous experiment once again but add to it a second factor. In addition to the amount of exposure to the model, the researcher decides to investigate the effects of the gender of the model on the amount of time children spend imitating the peer's behavior. Eight groups of subjects are now required—four groups observe a male model for each of the different exposure times, and four groups observe a female model. We would describe this study as a two-factor design with four levels of one variable and two levels of the other. Consider the potential results presented in Table 5.4. The raw scores (Table 5.4a) have been summarized for each of the eight *cells* (sets of scores representing unique combinations of the various levels of each factor). The means for each cell are presented in Table 5.4b. Note that the means have also been calculated for different combinations of groups—the scores of the males and females have been combined for each of the four exposure conditions, and the means calculated on each (4.0, 6.9, 13.5, 18.9); and the scores from the four exposure conditions have been combined for males and females (9.8, 11.9).

At this point, we can almost treat the experiment as if it were two separate investigations. By temporarily ignoring the

TABLE 5.4
Amount of Imitation (Group 2)

		Exposure (Minutes)			
		1	5	15	30
		1	3	10	15
		2	8	7	20
		6	2	9	18
	Male	3	6	3	30
	Model	5	9	11	22
		3	4	17	23
		2	5	16	21
		1	5	6	20
(a)		1	5	6	20
Raw Scores		2	6	8	24
		4	9	14	20
		8	11	15	18
		7	12	12	21
	Female	5	10	17	15
	Model	3	8	20	17
		6	7	18	16
		5	10	22	19
		2	9	19	12
		5	6	15	15
		6	8	17	13

		1	5	15	30	
(b)	Male Model	3.0	4.9	10.1	21.2	9.8
Mean Scores	Female Model	5.1	9.0	16.9	16.6	11.9
		4.0	6.9	13.5	18.9	

		F	Minimum F Value to Reject Null Hypothesis
(c)	Exposure	101.60	2.72
F Values	Gender of Model	10.08	3.98

		F	Minimum F Value to Reject Null Hypothesis
(d)	Exposure X		
Interaction	Gender of Model	13.52	2.72

male-female model variable, we can simply examine the results of the exposure variable on our dependent measure. Once again, a functional relationship seems apparent—greater exposure tends to result in increased imitation of the behavior. We can also examine the gender-of-the-model manipulation independently of the exposure variable. The means for these two levels indicate that the female model is imitated for longer periods of time than the male.

These data could be analyzed using an analysis of variance that would calculate separate F values for each of the variables (Table 5.4c). These values are considerably greater than those necessary to reject the null hypothesis, indicating a functional relationship between amount of imitation and both exposure time and the gender of the model.

Interaction Effects

If the multiple-factor design did nothing more than permit us to investigate a number of independent variables in the same study, it would be a valuable method. But this design also allows us to examine an additional important characteristic of the results—*interactions.* These are the unique effects of different combinations of the independent variables on the dependent measure. These combined effects often lead to different results from those expected if the variables were investigated separately. The analysis of variance procedure also calculates an F value for the interaction of the two variables. This value indicates the likelihood that the scores in each cell would have occurred given the separate, independent effects of the two variables.

In our study the interaction effect is also statistically significant (Table 5.4d). The easiest way to understand the source of an interaction is to graph the data. In Figure 5.1, the mean scores of the subjects observing the male and female models are presented visually for each of the four levels of the exposure variables. If there were no interaction in the results, the two lines would be parallel, indicating that each level of one variable had the same effect at all levels of the other variable. It is

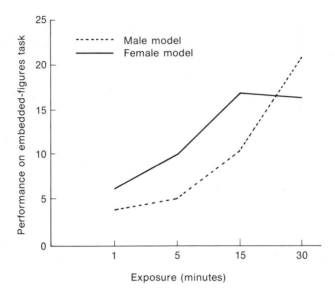

FIGURE 5.1
Results of a hypothetical experiment illustrating a statistical interaction. The effects of the two variables produce a unique result at the thirty-minute level of the independent variable.

clear from the graph that an interaction exists. Note that the scores with the male model continue to increase with greater amounts of exposure. But the scores with the female model do not increase beyond the fifteen-minute-level of exposure. The combination of the thirty-minute exposure time and the observation of a female model interact to produce results in the cell that do not fit the simple pattern suggested by separately considering the overall effects of the two variables. Interactions can take a variety of other forms as well, but they always indicate unusual effects produced when particular levels of two variables are considered.

Other Factorial Designs

There is actually no limit to the possible size of a factorial design. A study might consist of, for example, four factors with

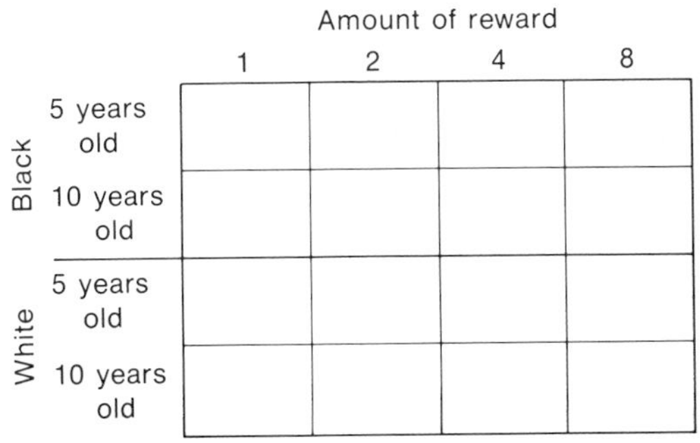

Amount of reward

FIGURE 5.2
A mixed factorial design involving three factors
(amount of reward, age, and race). Age and race
are between-subject factors, and amount of
reward is a within-subject factor.

three levels of each variable. In this case, the number of experimental cells would be eighty-one ($3 \times 3 \times 3 \times 3$). For
practical purposes, then, the number of subjects required in a
large factorial experiment often makes it very difficult to use.
The amount of information potentially obtainable, however,
can be quite extensive.

Multiple-factor designs can also involve repeated measures on one or more factors. In our example, if one group of
subjects observed a male model under the four exposure conditions, and a second group observed the female model under the
four exposure conditions, the experiment would have involved
a *mixed design*. That is, one factor (exposure) involved a
within-subject comparison, whereas the other factor (gender of
the model) involved a between-subject comparison.

Figure 5.2 illustrates a three-factor mixed design with four
levels of the first factor (amount of reward) and two levels of
the second and third factors (race and age). The design includes
repeated measures on the first factor. Note that all possible
combinations of the independent variables are represented, resulting in sixteen experimental cells. Factorial designs possessing this characteristic are called *orthogonal* designs; they offer
the most efficient manner of examining the separate and combined effects of a number of variables.

Conclusion

The experimental method, including the various designs discussed in this chapter, offers an extremely systematic and rigorous way of studying children's behavior. We have considered only a few of the major experimental designs and statistical methods, but even with these techniques the number of questions and issues that can be addressed seems virtually endless.

Yet, in the midst of this experimental precision, one aspect of the scientific approach may be becoming increasingly clear. Despite the rigor of our research procedures, the advanced technology of our experimental apparatus, and the sophistication of our statistical techniques, much of the experimental process remains uncomfortably vague. We are forced to make assumptions regarding the nature of the population, the representativeness of our samples, and the assignment of subjects to experimental conditions. And our results lead only to conclusions that offer acceptable levels of uncertainty.

It is important, therefore, that we continue not only to accumulate information using our current techniques, but to develop even more sophisticated methods of study. Undoubtedly there is much more left to be discovered about ways to study human behavior than we have revealed so far.

6 Time-Series Research

The third general approach to research we shall consider are the time-series designs. These methods are actually forms of experimental research, and most of the procedural principles discussed in the last chapter apply here as well. But the time-series approach has been developed and used primarily in applied areas, such as in clinical or educational settings, and its historical roots are distinct from the previous methods we have discussed. Much of the research in *applied behavior analysis* and *behavior modification* is conducted using these techniques.

Rationale

Time-series designs incorporate features of both the short-term experimental approach and the longitudinal approach. Time-series designs combine systematic manipulation of variables (typical of traditional experimental research) with the focus on behavior change in the individual that is characteristic of the longitudinal approach (Sidman, 1960).

Traditional experimental studies often demonstrate functional relationships between independent and dependent variables by comparing an experimental and a control group. The

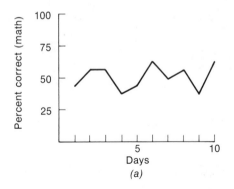

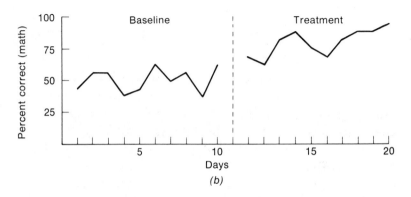

FIGURE 6.1
Results of a time-series experiment illustrating initial baseline data *(a)* and increase in performance following implementation of the treatment condition *(b)*.

experimental group subjects are exposed to the variable of interest, and the control group subjects are not. Differences between the performance of these groups on the dependent measure indicate the effects of the manipulated variable. The time-series approach is somewhat different. Functional relationships are demonstrated by systematically presenting and withholding the independent variable for the same individuals and observing changes in the dependent variable. If the behavior under study changes as a function of the presence or absence of the manipulated variable, a functional relationship can be assumed. Thus, subjects serve as both their own experimental and control groups.

Consider the following example. A school psychologist is interested in the effects of detailed feedback on a student's mathematical skills. In this study, mathematical performance is the dependent variable; in time-series research it often is called the *target behavior*. To examine this question, the psychologist first decides to determine the student's initial level of mathematical performance. Each day for two weeks, the teacher records the student's math scores and graphs them as in Figure 6.1a. The purpose of this initial period is to establish the level of the target behavior in the absence of the experimental variable (detailed feedback). This initial level of performance is called the subject's base level, or alternatively, the *baseline phase* of the experiment. Generally, baseline observations are continued until a reasonably stable level of performance is displayed. When this stabilization has occurred, the *treatment phase* of the study is introduced. The psychologist now instructs the teacher to add detailed feedback to the student's daily math reports. After each math assignment is graded, the teacher returns it to the student with detailed comments on why the student's answers were incorrect and how the correct answers could have been obtained. The teacher continues to record the student's daily math scores as before. The data from both phases are presented in Figure 6.1b. The student's math performance appears to improve very quickly with the introduction of the feedback manipulation. In fact, it is tempting to assert that a functional relationship between the two variables has now been demonstrated. But it is still too early for this conclusion.

The change in the target behavior seems to have corresponded to the manipulation of the feedback variable, but it could have been the result of other factors. It is not necessary to guess precisely what these other causes might have been; the point is that the behavior may have been improved regardless of the experimental treatment, and their correspondence may have been merely a coincidence. To appropriately demonstrate a functional relationship, the psychologist must proceed further.

Reversal (Withdrawal) Design

What actually is required in this situation is a *replication* of the previous demonstration. If presenting the feedback treatment improves mathematical performance, then withdrawing it and presenting it again should show a similar pattern of results. It is through such systematic replication that the time-series designs satisfy the requirements of scientific explanation.

The next phase necessary in the experiment, then, would be to return to the original baseline procedures. The teacher no longer includes detailed feedback with the math reports but simply proceeds as before. The results of this procedure are presented as the *reversal*, or *withdrawal phase*, of the experiment (Figure 6.2a). When the feedback variable is withdrawn, the behavior gradually returns to the original base level. In Figure 6.2b, the feedback treatment is reinstated (*Treatment II*), and the student's math performance rapidly returns to a high level.

The dependent measure has now been demonstrated to vary predictably as the independent variable is systematically presented and removed. At this point, the psychologist can claim to have demonstrated a functional relationship. Note that the two criteria discussed in Chapter 1 have been met. The psychologist can accurately *predict* the relationship between the independent and dependent variables and, using manipulative experimental procedures, can demonstrate *control* over this relationship.

The design we have just considered is sometimes called an A-B-A-B design. Each letter represents a different experimental treatment—in this case, A represents the baseline procedures, and B represents the treatment procedures. The psychologist could have continued alternating the experimental conditions (A-B-A-B-A-B), but the results are so clear that this is unnecessary. This last point is important. One characteristic of time-series research is that traditional statistical methods are infrequently used to analyze the data. Much more emphasis has been placed on "visual inspection" of the patterns in the data. This approach requires that the necessary trends in the data are clearly evident to any observer. We shall return to this issue later in the chapter.

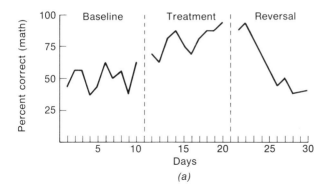

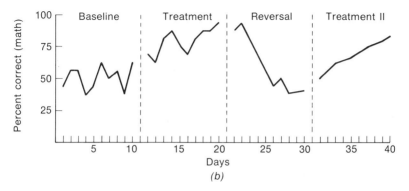

FIGURE 6.2
A time-series experiment with a reversal (withdrawal) of treatment
procedures *(a)* and introduction of a second phase of treatment *(b)*.

In the example just presented, the effects of one independent variable were examined. This design is the equivalent of a single-factor experimental design (detailed feedback) with two levels of the independent variable (presence or absence). It is also possible to use time-series methods to examine, in a single study, a number of variables—either separately or in combination.

For example, suppose the school psychologist decides also to investigate the effects of a second treatment—teacher praise. Each time the teacher returns a math assignment, rather than including detailed feedback on the student's performance, a

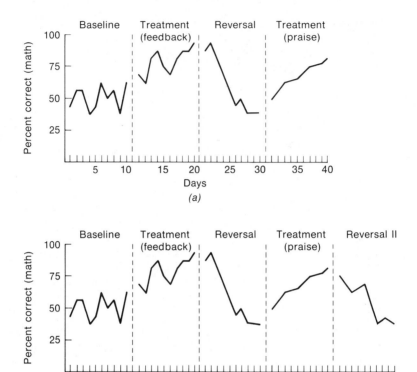

FIGURE 6.3
A time-series experiment illustrating evaluation of two different treatment procedures, including appropriate reversal phases.

statement praising the student's effort and perseverance is added to the report. If this variable were incorporated in the first study, it probably would have been introduced following the reversal phase. Figure 6.3a illustrates some hypothetical data from this variable. Again, the treatment appears to have improved math performance, but it is still necessary to demonstrate this effect clearly by introducing another return to baseline procedures (Figure 6.3b). This experiment would be called an A-B-A-C-A design.

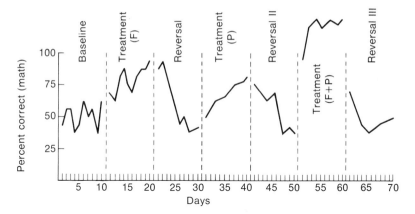

FIGURE 6.4
Evaluation of two separate treatment procedures followed by their use in combination.

Because both of these experimental manipulations worked so well, the psychologist decides to combine them into a single intervention treatment. Each math assignment now carries both detailed feedback and praise comments from the teacher. These results and the subsequent reversal procedures are presented in Figure 6.4; this would constitute an **A-B-A-C-A-BC-A** design. Note that the student's performance was better than when either treatment was presented separately. That is, the combination of the treatments seems to have produced an "additive" effect. With the time-series design, it is also possible to identify unique changes in behavior resulting from particular combinations of treatments. Recall from Chapter 5 that these are called *interactions*. For example, the data from the combined treatments might have been no different from their separate effects (Figure 6.5a), or data from the combined treatments might even have been lower than for either of the individual treatments (Figure 6.5b). Again, the causes of such interactions are not always immediately apparent and may require additional research. But they can be very important and should not be ignored.

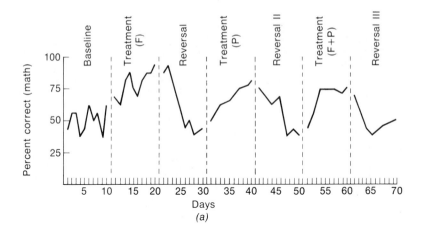

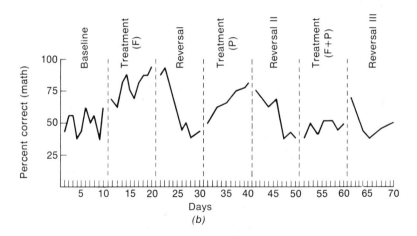

FIGURE 6.5
Illustration of two forms of treatment interaction. In the first (*a*), the combination of treatments (F + P) has no greater effect on performance than either of the separate treatments. In the second (*b*), the combination of the treatments is even less effective than either of the components.

The reversal design can thus accomplish many of the same experimental goals as between-group factorial designs. Most of the same procedural precautions apply here as well. For instance, a very important experimental requirement of the reversal design is that each treatment involve a change in only one variable at a time. In this way, clear functional relationships between a specific independent variable and the target behavior can be identified. If the psychologist in our example had begun by immediately introducing the combined feedback-praise manipulation, it would have been impossible to determine whether observed changes in the student's math performance were the result of one variable, the other, or their combination.

Multiple-Baseline Design

The reversal design is the most popular of the time-series methods. But there are times when it cannot easily be used, or is deemed undesirable for other reasons. Let us return to our example.

It is possible that the math performance of the student would not have followed the pattern we presented. The behavior could have improved as a result of the feedback manipulation (Figure 6.1b), but when the treatment was withdrawn, performance may not have declined as suggested (Figure 6.2a). The form of learning that occurred during the treatment may have been relatively permanent. That is, the student may have acquired math skills that were not immediately lost when the feedback procedures ended. Such *nonreversible effects* make the reversal design inappropriate in these circumstances. Alternatively, the psychologist may have decided that the desirable improvements in the student's math performance should not be reversed, even temporarily, simply for experimental purposes (see Chapter 11 for more on this issue).

In these cases, the reversal design can be replaced with an alternative time-series technique known as the *multiple-baseline design* (Baer, Wolf, and Risley, 1968). The rationale for this approach is somewhat different. Rather than demonstrating functional relationships by presenting and removing the independent variable, this design involves the successive (one-after-another) introduction of the variable under different conditions. Functional relationships are demonstrated if changes in behavior repeatedly correspond with the presentation of the experimental variable.

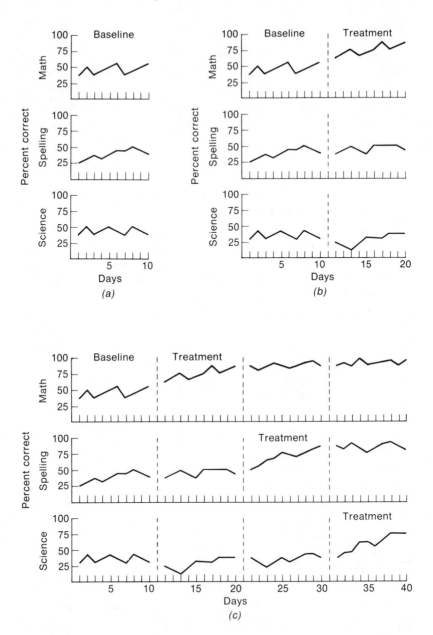

FIGURE 6.6
A multiple-baseline experiment studied across three academic behaviors. During the baseline period (a), there is no intervention. Next, treatment is introduced for only one behavior (b), and then it is introduced successively for the other two (c).

There are three principal forms of the multiple-baseline design. One is the *multiple-baseline across behaviors*. In this form, several behaviors are selected as potential targets. Baseline data are collected for each, and then the experimental treatment is successively applied to each. If a change in the behavior occurs each time the variable is introduced, a functional relationship can be assumed.

The school psychologist in our example might have begun by collecting baseline data on three different academic behaviors—math, spelling, and science (Figure 6.6a). After relatively stable base rates were observed, the feedback variable would be introduced only for the math behavior, but all three would continue to be monitored (Figure 6.6b). Following an improvement on that behavior, the treatment would be applied successively to the other behaviors. Figure 6.6c presents the data from a successful multiple-baseline intervention. These results are sufficient to infer a functional relationship between the feedback variable and the various academic behaviors.

Two other forms of multiple-baseline designs are frequently employed. *Multiple-baseline across subjects* involves the application of the treatment to a number of different subjects, as illustrated in Figure 6.7. Note that the experimental variable is not applied simultaneously to each but is delayed for a short period. This is a precaution against some other common factor suddenly improving the performance of all three subjects at the same time. Again, changes in the performance of each subject correspond to the introduction of the treatment and reveal a functional relationship.

Finally, similar questions can be investigated using a *multiple-baseline across settings* design. This approach involves applying the independent variable in different locations in much the same way as we have described with the two previous methods. For example, if the "teacher praise" variable was examined in the classroom, library, and cafeteria, with student cooperation as the target behavior, typical results might appear as in Figure 6.8.

The multiple-baseline design is not as useful as the reversal design, because it is often more difficult to draw firm conclusions from it. What could have been concluded if the

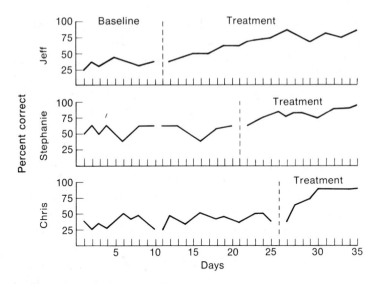

FIGURE 6.7
Multiple-baseline across subjects. Treatment is successively
introduced for each child, with corresponding changes in behavior
indicating a functional relationship.

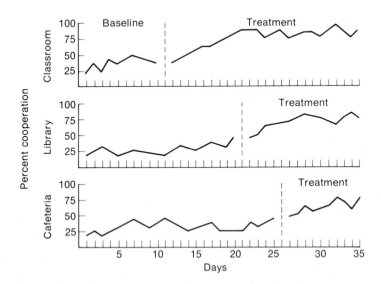

FIGURE 6.8
Multiple-baseline across settings.

feedback for math had also improved spelling performance (Figure 6.6b)? Perhaps the primary function of the treatment was that it prompted the student to pay greater attention to all schoolwork and take learning more seriously. If this effect generalized to other course work, it certainly would not mean that a functional relationship between feedback and math did not exist. Instead, it simply would indicate that the multiple-baseline design was not adequate to unambiguously discover this relationship.

The multiple-baseline design is thus most useful when a particular pattern of results emerges. That is, behavior changes must clearly correspond to the successive presentations of the treatment condition. As the pattern of results becomes less clear than this, the value of this time-series design quickly decreases.

Changing-Criterion Design

A second alternative to the reversal design has been developed, and it too eliminates the necessity of reinstating undesirable behavior. In the *changing-criterion design*, the functional relationship between the treatment and the behavior is established by systematically increasing what is required of the subject (Hartmann and Hall, 1976).

The procedure begins with a baseline phase on the single target behavior of interest. Once sufficient stability has been demonstrated, the treatment is introduced. Behavior problems suitable for this form of design are typically those where gradual, step-like changes may occur. Treatment often involves rewarding specific amounts of behavior change. When the treatment is first introduced, the criterion amount of change necessary to receive reward may be rather modest. When this change in behavior has occurred, the criterion is then raised to demand additional change for obtaining reward. This procedure continues until the behavior reaches an acceptable level.

For example, Figure 6.9 illustrates the results of a hypothetical case employing this design. A child has continually expressed interest in learning to play a musical instru-

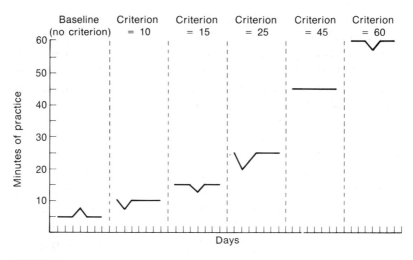

FIGURE 6.9
A changing-criterion design. As the target behavior increases, the criterion
necessary for reward is gradually increased. The pattern of behavior-changes
confirms the effectiveness of treatment.

ment, but several attempts by the parents to encourage this
pursuit have failed because the child has difficulty sitting down
to practice each day. To help develop this habit, the child
agrees to a plan whereby the opportunity to watch television
each night would be earned by a given amount of practice on
the saxophone. At first, the child is required to practice for ten
minutes each day to earn that evening's television time. When
this level is clearly established, the criterion is raised to fifteen
minutes per day. Eventually, the child practices for one hour
every afternoon. The corresponding improvement in skill
makes practice so enjoyable that the reward becomes unnecessary.

The changing-criterion design is somewhat preferable to
the multiple-baseline design because it can be used with a
single child and a single behavior in a single setting. This may
be crucial in situations where multiple baselines cannot easily
be obtained. However, this design shares an important disadvantage. To establish a firm, functional relationship between
the treatment and the behavior, changes in the behavior must
closely correspond to the pattern of changes in the criterion. If

this correspondence does not occur, greater uncertainty is introduced into the conclusions.

Other Characteristics

It may be useful to describe several other important features of time-series designs. To begin, we shall compare them with the between-groups experimental approach on several dimensions.

Comparisons with Between-Groups Designs

One obvious difference between these two approaches is the number of subjects required to conduct an investigation. In the between-groups approach, it is necessary to have relatively large numbers of subjects in each condition to guarantee a representative sample and to improve the chances of finding treatment effects. The time-series design can employ very few subjects or even a single subject, because each subject essentially constitutes a separate experiment.

A second major difference is that the results of time-series research reflect the effects of an experimental manipulation on an actual subject. In between-groups studies, the data in each condition are averaged, and treatment differences reflect the "typical" subject studied under those conditions. Occasionally, the data can actually fail to represent *any* single subject. For example, if all the subjects exposed to one level of an independent variable score either very high or very low, the mean for this group will lie somewhere between these extremes where no subject actually scored.

One potential problem with employing very few subjects, however, is the issue of the *generalizability* of the findings. As we saw in Chapter 2, experiments are conducted on only a sample of subjects, but the results are ultimately generalized to a larger population. When a single subject (or only several) are used to examine the effects of a treatment, it is necessary to guard against the possibility that an untypical subject will produce very uncharacteristic results. In our earlier example, if the subject had not responded to the feedback manipulation, we might have concluded that it was not generally a very good technique. Yet, further research might have demonstrated that nine of ten children improve under this experimental treatment. For some purposes, such as a clinical intervention to aid a specific child, generalizability is much less important. What matters in such a case is to establish that the treatment does or does not work for that child. But in most psychological investigations, the ability confidently to apply specific data to the larger population is a crucial aspect of the research.

One disadvantage of the time-series approach is the amount of time required to conduct a study. In between-groups designs, the data can often be collected very quickly. Subjects usually can be studied under the various experimental conditions with little or no regard for time. Time-series research, in contrast, frequently involves daily, or at least periodic, observations and successive presentations of the various phases of treatment. Such research may continue for weeks or months.

Statistical Versus Meaningful Change

There has been a continuing debate over the value and necessity of statistical methods in time-series research. The most compelling argument favoring the use of these methods is that observed differences in behavior which seem to be related to the experimental manipulations may simply be within the range of chance variability. Statistical techniques provide this kind of information and help the investigator to reach reasonable conclusions regarding the data.

But the problem is usually not that time-series researchers are too quick to accept behavior-change as evidence of functional relationships. It is more likely that they are unwilling to accept statistical evidence of change as meaningful. This issue arises because these researchers are often involved in applied intervention research rather than more basic investigations.

Consider the following example. A researcher wants to develop a program to increase the rate of vocabulary acquisition in slow readers. The average rate among the other children in this class is 10.6 new words per week; the rate among the slow readers is .8 words per week. The investigator introduces an eight-week program of intensive training with the lower group and finds that their acquisition rate eventually climbs to 1.2 words. Because almost all the subjects improved at least a small amount, and because a reasonably large number of subjects was involved in the program, this increase proves to be a statistically significant change. That is, the improvement can be attributed to the intervention program with a reasonable degree of certainty. This satisfies the requirement for demonstrating a functional relationship, but the investigator does not consider the project a success.

In this case, the time and effort invested in the program did not result in a level of change that would be considered meaningful or important *for practical purposes*. Perhaps from a theoretical point of view it indicates that the subjects were capable of improvement and that components of the program were sufficient to cause this change. But the size of the improvement may be deemed inadequate on more pragmatic grounds.

There is no simple solution to this debate. We have seen that determining the significance of change, in a statistical sense, involves a good deal of arbitrary decision-making. This is even more the case when the meaningfulness of change is at issue. But the issue illustrates that the criteria used to evaluate the results of a study cannot easily be separated from the ultimate purposes of the research.

Statistical tests are sometimes included in time-series research, and in fact this trend seems to be increasing (Kazdin, 1976). But there remains an obvious commitment to maintaining the appropriate perspective on these techniques. They do not provide simple answers, but only additional information for the investigator to evaluate.

Conclusion

Time-series designs offer a very useful combination of characteristics for the research psychologist. They permit analysis of the effects of an independent variable on the behavior of an individual subject. They can also be used to examine functional relationships, which may be generalized to much larger populations. For the therapist or applied investigator, the time-series approach has proved to be a most important research technique for both assessment and modification of children's behavior.

The research designs we have considered in the last three chapters comprise the major approaches to research with children. Almost all research investigations can be characterized by one of the designs outlined in this unit. In the next unit, we shall consider more specific research techniques and strategies of investigation.

References

Baer, D. M., Wolf, M. M., and Risley, R. Some current dimensions of applied behavior analysis. *Journal of Applied Behavior Analysis,* 1968, **1,** 91–97.

Hartmann, D. P., and Hall, R. V. The changing criterion design. *Journal of Applied Behavior Analysis,* 1976, **9,** 527–532.

Kazdin, A. E. Statistical analyses for single-case experimental designs. In M. Herson and D. H. Barlow (eds.), *Single-Case experimental designs: Strategies for studying behavior change.* New York: Pergamon Press, 1976.

Sidman, M. *Tactics of scientific research.* New York: Basic Books, 1960.

III

Tactics of
Investigation

7 Basic Measures of Behavior

In the previous chapters, we have discussed the scientific approach to the study of the child and outlined the basic research designs useful for investigating questions in this area. We now begin to consider a number of research procedures and techniques employed by child researchers. Our review of these procedures must be selective, because the number of different specific methods is very large. To simplify the task, we have organized this chapter, and the next, according to those types of dependent variables, or measures of behavior, that child psychologists most frequently study.

The selection of the appropriate behavioral measure is an extremely important decision for the researcher. Every response possesses a number of characteristics—its strength, its variability, its correspondence with other responses, and so on. Sometimes an independent variable may be functionally related to the behavior under study, but the relationship is only apparent with a few of these characteristics. For example, in Chapter 2 we saw that the source of reward can affect the size of the child's contribution to a charity (magnitude of the response). However, there may be no relationship between the source of reward and the speed with which the child decides to make the contribution (latency of the response). In fact, the same independent variable can sometimes affect one characteristic of the behavior in one direction and a second characteristic in a different direction. For these reasons, the measure of the behavior must be carefully selected to address the particular question(s) of interest. In this chapter we shall describe several basic measures of behavior and then, in Chapter 8, discuss more complex measures and various research techniques associated with them.

The measures of behavior presented in this chapter are considered *basic* because they are concerned primarily with characteristics of the response (behavior) in its own right. These characteristics include how often the behavior is displayed (frequency and rate), how intensely the behavior occurs (magnitude), how quickly the behavior is produced (latency), and how long the behavior lasts (duration). In contrast, the more complex measures of behavior, discussed in the following chapter, involve relationships between the response and other aspects of the situation, such as other behaviors or events.

As we describe each measure, a number of actual studies will be presented to illustrate its use. In some cases, we have simplified our presentation of the procedures or results to eliminate irrelevant information. The interested reader is encouraged to read these reports in their original published form (see Chapter 12).

Frequency

Perhaps the most widely used measure of behavior is the total number of occurrences of the behavior. A psychologist interested in determining the frequency of a response would simply arrange to count the number of times the behavior is displayed. The most important aspect of this procedure is defining the behavior clearly enough so that there is no question as to its occurrence or nonoccurrence. We shall consider this issue again in Chapter 10. Two studies illustrate the use of frequency counts.

Bandura and Perloff (1967) compared the effects of different reward systems on children's frequency of performing an effortful task. The task for all children was to turn a wheel to accumulate points on a game-like apparatus. The children were

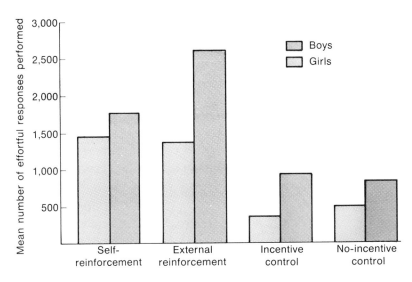

FIGURE 7.1
Mean number of turning responses for boys and girls in each experimental condition. (From A. Bandura and B. Perloff. Relative efficacy of self-monitored and externally imposed reinforcement systems. *Journal of Personality and Social Psychology*, 1967, **7**, 111–116. Copyright © 1967 by the American Psychological Association. Reprinted by permission.)

randomly assigned to one of four treatment conditions (four levels of the independent variable). The children either (a) rewarded themselves for the wheel-turning responses (self-reward), (b) received reward for the responses from the experimenter (external reward), (c) received reward before the turning began (incentive control), or (d) received no reward (no incentive control). The measure of interest was the frequency (total number) of turning responses produced by the child. The results of this study are presented in Figure 7.1; they indicate that both self-reward and external reward produced a greater frequency of effortful responses than either control condition. Also, males produced more responses than females in each condition.

A second study involving frequency counts was conducted in a rehabilitation center for "predelinquent" adolescents (Phillips, 1968). In an attempt to improve the verbal behavior of the

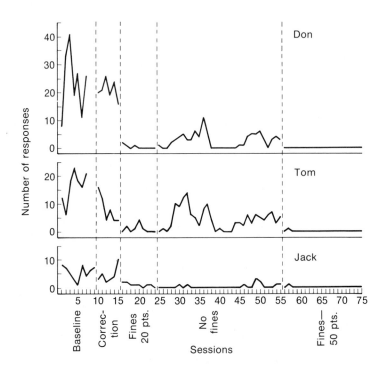

FIGURE 7.2
Number of aggressive statements per three-hour session for each youth
under each condition. (From E. L. Phillips. Achievement Place: Token
reinforcement procedures in a home-style rehabilitation setting for
"pre-delinquent" boys. *Journal of Applied Behavior Analysis*, 1968, **1**,
213–223. Copyright © 1968 by the Society for the Experimental
Analysis of Behavior, Inc. Reprinted by permission.)

youths, the investigators compared two systems for reducing
aggressive statements. The frequency of these behaviors was
examined during a three-hour period each day, using a time-
series design. After a baseline of aggressive statements was
collected for one week, a procedure was introduced involving
simple verbal reprimands for the target responses (correction).
This procedure had only moderate success in reducing the
frequency of aggressive statements. A second procedure followed, in which deductions were made from points that the
youths had earned to obtain special privileges (fines). As can be
seen in Figure 7.2, the fines were effective in reducing the

number of responses for two of the youths, but the improvement was not entirely maintained if the fines were removed.

A special case of the frequency-count method is when the psychologist is concerned only with the presence or absence of a behavior—that is, when the data are essentially 1 or 0 for each subject. An example of this approach is a study by Flavell, Beach, and Chinsky (1966) concerned with children's memory abilities. Subjects were asked to recall a number of pictures that had been presented, removed, and rearranged. One important measure in this experiment was whether children displayed evidence of silently "rehearsing" the original positions of the pictures when they were absent. The measure of interest was the presence or absence of lip movements by the children. The investigators found that the use of this behavior became more common as older subjects were observed.

Rate

A measure of behavior very much related to frequency is rate—that is, the number of times a behavior occurs *per unit of time.* For example, a school psychologist may have less interest in the total number of times a child cries than in the number of times the behavior occurs each hour or day. Rate measures are also frequently used when the question involves the acquisition or learning of a new behavior.

An example of a rate measure can be found in a study by Bloom and Esposito (1975). These psychologists were interested in the relationship between infant vocalizations and social stimulation in the infant's environment. In particular, they wished to compare social stimulation that was contingent on the vocalizations (that is, it only was presented following a vocalization) versus the same amount of stimulation presented in a noncontingent, unrelated fashion. The measure they selected was the number of vocalizations the child produced each minute over a twelve-minute experimental session. Using a time-series design, they first obtained a baseline level of vocalizations without social stimulation. Next, for one group of infants, each vocalization was followed by a smile from the

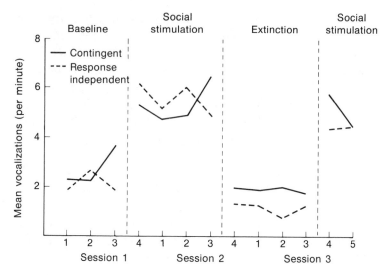

FIGURE 7.3
Mean vocalization rate for infants in each condition. (From K. Bloom and A.
Esposito. Social conditioning and its proper control procedures. *Journal of
Experimental Child Psychology*, 1975, **19**, 209–222. Copyright © 1975 by
Academic Press, Inc. Reprinted by permission.)

experimenter, a touch on the infant's abdomen, and a "tsk, tsk,
tsk" sound (contingent social stimulation). The remaining infants were given the same amount of stimulation, but it was
"yoked" to the stimulation received by the other subjects. That
is, the noncontingent group received their stimulation at the
same times that the other group received it, but not necessarily
always following an infant vocalization. The purpose of these
procedures was to determine whether the simple presence of
social stimulation would increase vocalizations, or whether a
particular relationship between the stimulation and behavior
was required. (Yoking procedures are used to keep all aspects
of the situation the same for each group, except the particular
aspect of interest. In this case, the amount and timing of the
stimulation were kept constant for all subjects, but the "contingency" of the relationship was different.) Following the
treatment phase, all stimulation was removed, then subse-

quently reinstated in the final phase (Figure 7.3). It is apparent from the data that both forms of social stimulation increased the rate of infant vocalizations, and that the contingency between the stimulation and the response was not particularly important.

One experiment that illustrates the relationship between rate and frequency measures is a single-subject case report (Whitehurst, Novak, and Zorn, 1972). A three-and-one-half-year-old child was referred to the psychologists because he produced only a few words, although apparently normal in all other areas. The strategy employed to deal with this problem involved changing the mother's verbal behavior toward the child. Two classes of maternal speech were systematically varied—*prompts* (attempts to encourage imitation by labeling objects and asking the child to repeat the labels) and *conversation* (asking the child questions and giving verbal responses to the child's comments). These classes of speech constituted the independent variable. The characteristic of the child's behavior that was measured was the number of new words produced each day. Figure 7.4 depicts the child's production of new words under several combinations of variations in the mother's speech.

The particular manner of graphing these data is known as a *cumulative record*. As usual, the horizontal axis indicates the sessions (days, trials) during which different levels of the independent variable are presented. On the vertical axis are the *cumulative* number of responses produced during the study. That is, each session's data represent the total number of responses that have occurred in the experiment up to and including that time. Because each point represents a total of all that has come before, the slope of the graph can only go up or remain the same; it can never go down. If the behavior is produced at a very low rate, the slope of the graph will be almost flat; if the behavior is produced at a high rate, the slope will become very steep. For example, the subject produced very few new words each day during the first phase (low conversation, low prompts), but the rate of new responses increased markedly during the second phase (high conversation, high prompts). In fact, either prompting or conversation was effec-

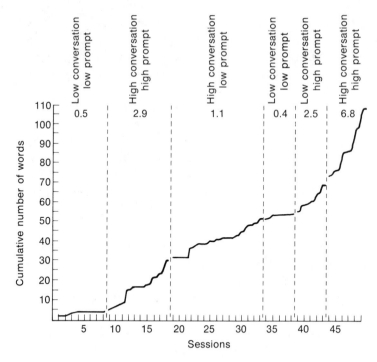

FIGURE 7.4
Cumulative number of new words produced by the child during each session. (From G. J. Whitehurst et al. Delayed speech studied in the home. *Developmental Psychology*, 1972, **7**, 169–177. Copyright © 1972 by the American Psychological Association. Reprinted by permission.)

tive in increasing word production, and the combination of the two was the most effective.*

Magnitude

A third basic measure of behavior involves the size or intensity of the response. In this case, we are not concerned with the number of behaviors that are produced, but with a characteristic of each individual response.

---

*To be certain that the cumulative-record approach is understood, it may be helpful to redraw the graph using the more traditional method. The *average* number of new words acquired each session is indicated for each phase. Using

Investigations of children's sharing or altruistic behavior often use magnitude measures. In most cases, subjects are exposed to a particular treatment condition and then are given an opportunity to share their possessions with others (for example, donate them to a charity). In such studies, each child typically produces only one response. Therefore, the rate or frequency of the behavior is irrelevant. However, the magnitude of the response often can be shown to vary as a function of the independent variable manipulation. Moore, Underwood, and Rosenhan (1973), for example, found that the size of children's donations is related to the mood or emotional feelings they are experiencing at the time. One group of children was instructed to think happy thoughts; a second group was instructed to think sad thoughts; one control group simply counted silently; and a second control group received no particular instructions. The children thinking happy thoughts later donated more to the charity than either of the control groups, whereas the children thinking sad thoughts donated the least.

Magnitude of a response also refers to its strength or intensity. Physically aggressive responses, for example, can be measured according to these characteristics. In one investigation, children saw a filmed model punished for breaking a rule (Slaby and Parke, 1968). For one group of subjects, the film involved physical punishment (spanking) to the model, whereas a second group saw a film depicting the use of verbal explanation (reasoning) for the child's misbehavior. A control group saw no film. The researchers were interested in the degree to which the young viewers would be influenced by the film's disciplinary technique when put in such a situation. Following the film, all subjects were asked to help teach another child to do arithmetic problems by punishing the child's mistakes. The procedure involved having the subject turn a dial each time the child made an error. The dial supposedly delivered a punch to the child, who was working in the next room (although this, of course, did not actually take

this number as the actual amount produced during each session of the phase, a graph can be constructed similar to the one reported by Bloom and Esposito (1975) in Figure 7.3. This graph may better illustrate the relationship between the various levels of the independent variable and the child's behavior.

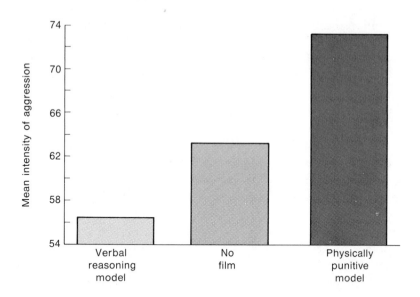

FIGURE 7.5
Mean intensity of aggressive dial responses for groups of children exposed to
different disciplinary models. (From R. D. Parke. Some effects of punishment
on children's behavior. Reprinted by permission from *The Young Child:
Reviews of Research*, vol. 2, edited by Willard W. Hartup, p. 280. Copyright
© 1972, National Association for the Education of Young Children, 1834
Connecticut Avenue, N.W., Washington, D.C. 20009, by permission.)

place). The dial apparatus was designed so that the intensity of
the subject's responses could be measured. A clear effect was
found in younger subjects, as illustrated in Figure 7.5. The
average intensity of the dial responses was very much related
to the previous film viewing condition.

Physiological responses are often studied with magnitude
measures. An excellent sample involves research on the habituation process. We shall postpone discussion of that technique,
however, until Chapter 9.

Duration

In addition to their intensity, some individual responses
can also be described by their duration. Explicit definitions of

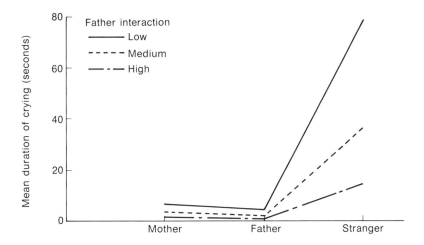

FIGURE 7.6
Duration of crying when infant is left alone with different categories of adults for three levels of reported father interaction. (From E. Spelke et al. Father interaction and separation protest. *Developmental Psychology*, 1973, **9**, 83–90. Copyright © 1973 by the American Psychological Association. Reprinted by permission.)

behavior again are important when using this measure, because the determination of where one response ends and the next one begins may not always be obvious. But, from another point of view, responses that are not easily separated may be more easily studied using a duration measure. Crying is a good example, as shown by the next study.

A duration measure of crying was examined in one-year-old infants as an indicator of their distress when in the company of a strange adult (Spelke, Zelazo, Kagan, and Kotelchuck, 1973). The researchers were specifically concerned with the role of the father in this process. Three groups of infants were formed—those whose fathers reported having much interaction with the infant, those whose father-infant interaction was at a moderate level, and those whose fathers indicated little interaction. All infants then were observed in a structured setting involving various combinations of the mother, father, or adult female stranger. The results of three of these test situations are presented in Figure 7.6. Not surprisingly, very little crying occurred when the infant was left alone with either its father or its mother. However, infants in all groups displayed distress when left with the stranger. It is obvious, however, that the degree of distress (duration of crying) is related to the amount of previous interaction with the father.*

An interesting use of a duration measure can be seen in a study by Mischel and Ebbesen (1970). These psychologists were investigating the factors that influence children's ability to delay gratification (pass up a small, immediate reward for a larger, delayed reward). In this study, the measure of the child's behavior was the duration of their waiting. This behavior may seem to be simply the absence of other behaviors, but in this case it can be viewed as an active, purposeful response. All subjects were instructed that they would be left alone to wait for the large reward, but that at any point they could signal the experimenter and receive the small reward, instead. Children were studied under one of four waiting conditions. For one group, both the small and large rewards were present in open view: for the second and third groups, either the large or small reward was present; the fourth group waited with neither reward in view. Somewhat to the surprise of the researchers, childen waited the longest when neither reward was present. They waited less when one or the other was present. And they waited least when both were present.

Latency

The final basic measure that we shall discuss also involves the element of time. In many situations, the important characteristic of the response is how quickly it occurs. Latency measures are frequently used in studies of perceptual or cognitive processes. Often they take the form of *reaction time*, or the ability to make the correct response as quickly as possible.

---

*It should be recalled that this study is not a "true" experiment, because infants were not randomly assigned to the various levels of the independent variable (father interaction), as discussed in Chapter 2. Therefore, it is possible that the amount of father-infant interaction was not the simple *cause* of the observed differences in behavior, but instead may have *resulted from* some characteristic of the infant that also produced the crying effect (e.g., irritability).

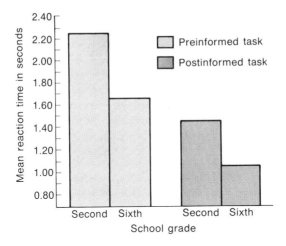

FIGURE 7.7
Reaction times for second and sixth graders for two
visual tasks. (From A. D. Pick and G. W. Frankel. A
study of strategies of visual attention in children.
Developmental Psychology, 1973, **9**, 348–357.
Copyright © 1973 by the American Psychological
Association. Reprinted by permission.)

To illustrate, Pick and Frankel (1973) examined children's
ability to make visual discriminations involving either the
shape or the size of two animal figures. The subject was seated
at an apparatus that had two buttons—one marked "Yes" (indicating that either the size or shape of the two stimuli were
the same), the other marked "No" (indicating that neither the
size nor shape was similar). For half of the trials, the experimenter presented a slide containing the two figures,
immediately announced "size" or "shape" as the relevant characteristic for that trial, and simultaneously started a clock (preinformed condition). As soon as the subjects determined whether
the cued characteristic was the same or different, they pushed
the appropriate button and stopped the clock. The elapsed time
between the presentation of the stimulus and the child's response (reaction time) was used as the measure of behavior.
For the remaining trials, the experimenter first presented the
slide for only one second. She then turned it off, announced the
relevant cue, and simultaneously started the clock (postin-

formed condition). Again, the measure of the behavior was the reaction time between the cue and the child's response. The data for this experiment are presented in Figure 7.7, which shows that the latencies for the older subjects were shorter (that is, they responded more quickly). This was true under both viewing conditions, although the preinformed task apparently was more difficult (longer latencies).

Latency also has been used to assess children's tolerance for violence (Drabman and Thomas, 1974). Third- and fourth-grade subjects were studied. Half of the subjects were first exposed to a short film portraying violence and aggression. The other subjects saw no film. All children were then brought to a room, where they were told that they could monitor a nearby room on a closed-circuit television. The experimenter explained that two younger children would soon be entering the monitored room and that the subject would be able to watch them on the television. The experimenter then left the room for a few minutes, but instructed the subject to come and get him if there was any trouble. As soon as the experimenter left, two young children came on the screen and shortly began to fight. The dependent measure in this study was how long the subject watching the children waited before summoning help. The study indicated that viewing a violent film increased the latency of seeking help—that is, those children took longer to respond. Note that this study is similar to that of Mischel and Ebbesen (1970) in that it also measured waiting time. But, in this case, the issue was more directly related to seeking help as the important behavior, rather than the waiting response. To some degree, however, this is simply a matter of emphasis, and it illustrates the flexible nature of these measures.

Conclusion

We have described five basic measures of behavior that researchers often use to study children. Our presentation may have implied that the psychologist must select only one measure of a behavior for use in a study. This is hardly the case. In fact, it is probably true that most published research investigations involve more than a single dependent measure. Frequently, several different questions can be addressed simply by considering different aspects of the same behavior. At other times, different measures may be used to get at the same question in different ways.

This issue raises an important point about scientific inquiry. Although research often may seem very precise and technical, it also involves a good deal of creativity and imagination on the part of the investigator. In many areas of child study, the questions are clear, but developing ways to answer them presents the greatest problem. As we proceed through the next two chapters, it may be useful to occasionally pause and consider how a particular study might have been approached somewhat differently—using a different research design or different measures of behavior—and still have produced the information necessary to answer the questions under investigation.

References

Bandura, A., and Perloff, B. Relative efficacy of self-monitored and externally imposed reinforcement systems. *Journal of Personality and Social Psychology*, 1967, **7**, 111–116.

Bloom, K., and Esposito, A. Social conditioning and its proper control procedures. *Journal of Experimental Child Psychology*, 1975, **19**, 209–222.

Drabman, R. S., and Thomas, M. H. Does media violence increase children's toleration of real-life aggression? *Developmental Psychology*, 1974, **10**, 418–421.

Flavell, J. H., Beach, D. R., and Chinsky, J. M. Spontaneous verbal rehearsal in a memory task as a function of age. *Child Development*, 1966, **37**, 283–299.

Mischel, W., and Ebbesen, E. B. Attention in delay of gratification. *Journal of Personality and Social Psychology*, 1970, **16**, 329–337.

Moore, B. S., Underwood, B., and Rosenhan, D. C. Affect and altruism. *Developmental Psychology*, 1973, **8**, 99–104.

Phillips, E. L. Achievement place: Token reinforcement procedures in a home-style rehabilitation setting for "pre-delinquent" boys. *Journal of Applied Behavior Analysis*, 1968, **1**, 213–223.

Pick, A. D., and Frankel, G. W. A study of strategies of visual attention in children. *Developmental Psychology*, 1973, **9**, 348–357.

Slaby, R. G., and Parke, R. D. The influence of a punitive or reasoning model on resistance to deviation and aggression in children (Cited in R. D. Parke. Some effects of punishment on children's behavior.) In W. W. Hartup (ed.), *The Young Child*. Washington, D.C.: National Association for the Education of Young Children, 1972, **2**, 264–283.

Spelke, E., Zelazo, P., Kagan, J., and Kotelchuck, M. Father interaction and separation protest. *Developmental Psychology*, 1973, **9**, 83–90.

Whitehurst, G. J., Novak, G., and Zorn, G. A. Delayed speech studied in the home. *Developmental Psychology*, 1972, **7**, 169–177.

8 Complex Measures and Techniques

The measures of behavior discussed in Chapter 7 involved only aspects of the response itself. We shall now consider a number of measures that are defined in relation to other stimuli or behaviors. These complex measures are often used within a particular *experimental paradigm*. A paradigm is a specific set of research procedures that can be adapted to study a variety of related research questions. Several important experimental paradigms will also be considered in conjunction with their particular measures of behavior.

Accuracy

The most common of the complex measures are concerned with the accuracy of the child's response. These measures are used in those situations where a correct response exists or where certain behaviors can be defined as incorrect. The manner of establishing which response is right or wrong depends on the experimental task being used. We shall describe three frequently used paradigms in which the accuracy of the response is the dependent measure under study.

Recall

The study of human memory abilities is usually investigated using a recall paradigm. Generally, this procedure involves presenting the child with a set of items or stimuli that the experimenter has arranged in a particular manner. The items then are removed, and the child is asked to recognize or reproduce them. The independent variables in these studies typically are concerned with identifying those factors that affect the accuracy of the child's responses. In this case, a response is defined as correct if it corresponds to the previous arrangement with which the subject was presented.

An example of this paradigm is found in a study by Brown and Murphy (1975). Four-year-old children were presented with a series of pictures, which involved either (a) an ordered story sequence, (b) a scrambled story sequence, or (c) a random group of items (Figure 8.1). The task involved having the subjects reproduce the order in which the pictures were presented. A second independent variable was the amount of lag between being presented with the stimuli and being asked to recall them. The results are presented in Figure 8.2. Note that no difference in accuracy exists between ordered and random items when testing occurs immediately following stimulus presentation. As the lag increases, however, the ordered items are reproduced consistently with more accuracy.

An interesting paradigm involving memory processes is concerned with *incidental learning*. These studies usually involve a task in which two sets of stimulus materials are presented simultaneously. Subjects are instructed to pay attention to one set of stimuli because they will later be tested on them. Performance with these stimuli represents the measure of *central* learning. No instructions are given regarding the other set of stimuli. Later, children are asked to recall characteristics of this second set. Performance with these materials indicates the degree of *incidental* learning.

Hale and Piper (1973) examined the relationship between the two sets of stimuli and its effects on children of different ages. Two tasks were used. In the pictures task, children were shown the stimuli presented in Figure 8.3a and were instructed to remember only one set of them (either animals or household

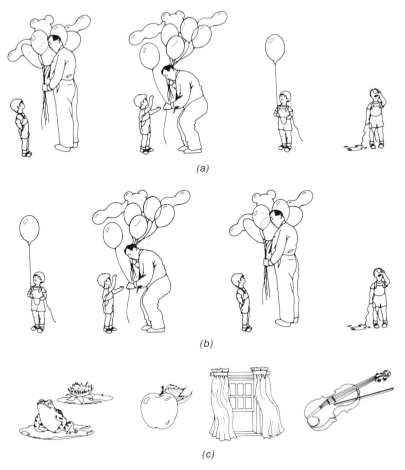

(a)

(b)

(c)

FIGURE 8.1
Stimulus materials representing an ordered story *(a)*, a scrambled story
(b), or a random series *(c)*. (From A.L. Brown and M.D. Murphy. Reconstruction
of arbitrary versus logical sequences by preschool children. *Journal of
Experimental Child Psychology*, 1975, **20**, 307–326. Copyright © 1975 by
Academic Press, Inc. Reprinted by permission.)

items). The stimuli then were removed, and children were
required to point to the previous position of an item from that
set as it was named. This performance constituted the central learning data. Children next were presented with one set
of the pictured items and asked to recall the item that had
appeared with it. These results indicated the amount of incidental learning.

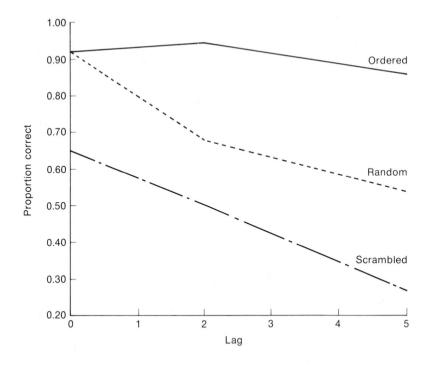

FIGURE 8.2
Mean proportion of correct orders for each of three types of stimulus for three
degrees of lag. (From A. L. Brown and M. D. Murphy. Reconstruction of
arbitrary versus logical sequences by preschool children. *Journal of
Experimental Child Psychology*, 1975, **20**, 307–326. Copyright © 1975 Academic
Press, Inc. Reprinted by permission.

The colored shapes task involved the same general procedures but employed the stimuli shown in Figure 8.3b—six
geometric shapes of six different colors. The central measure
involved learning the positions of either the shapes or colors,
and the incidental measure involved recalling the particular
color and shape combinations. The results of these two tasks on
the two measures of recall accuracy are presented in Table 8.1
for eight-year-old and twelve-year-old subjects. With the pictures task, the older children recalled more items of the central
set, but performed no better with the incidental stimuli. On the
colored shapes task, however, the older children performed
better on both measures of learning. The difference in results

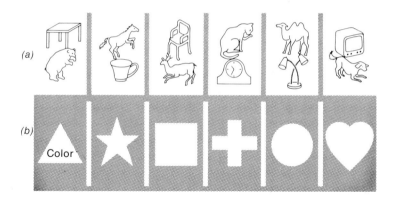

FIGURE 8.3
Stimuli used in pictures (a) and colored shapes (b) tasks. (From G. A. Hale and R. A. Piper. Developmental trends in children's incidental learning: Some critical stimulus differences. *Developmental Psychology,* 1973, **8,** 327–335. Copyright © 1973 by the American Psychological Association. Reprinted by permission.)

may be attributed to the degree to which each set of stimuli can be related as a single unit rather than as completely separated items.

Problem-Solving

Accuracy also refers to a child's ability to solve simple problems presented by the experimenter. In such cases a cor-

TABLE 8.1
Mean Scores on Two Tasks

Task	Central Learning		Incidental Learning	
	Age 8	Age 12	Age 8	Age 12
Pictures	3.70	6.40	1.70	1.75
Colored Shapes	4.15	6.45	1.45	3.30

Source: G. A. Hale and R. A. Piper. Developmental trends in children's incidental learning. *Developmental Psychology,* 1973, **8,** 327–335. Copyright © 1973 by the American Psychological Association. Reprinted by permission.

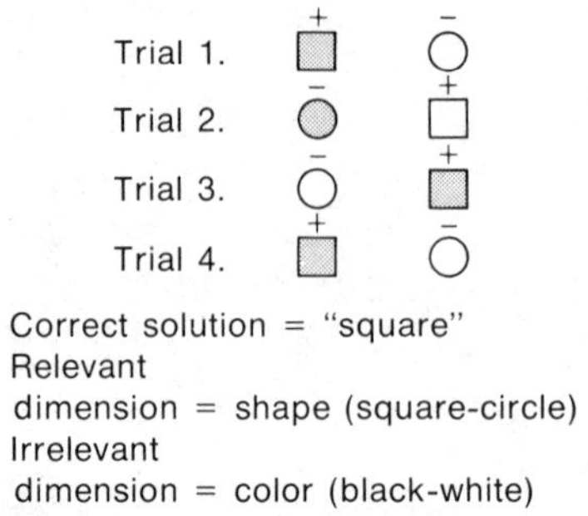

Trial 1.
Trial 2.
Trial 3.
Trial 4.

Correct solution = "square"
Relevant
dimension = shape (square-circle)
Irrelevant
dimension = color (black-white)

FIGURE 8.4
Four trials in a typical
concept-learning task. Correct
responses (+) and incorrect responses
(−) indicate that the concept to be
learned is "square." In this case,
shape is a relevant dimension for
solving the task, but color is not.

rect solution exists, and the subject's response is accurate if it corresponds to the solution.

One of the most frequently used problem-solving paradigms involves *concept-learning*. In these tasks, the child must learn to identify stimuli that have a common similarity—that is, form a concept. For example, in Figure 8.4, four such learning trials are illustrated. On each trial the child selects one stimulus and is informed whether it is correct or incorrect. At first, the child may make many errors, but eventually the concept is acquired. In the figure, the concept is "square," and only those responses are considered correct (+); responses to the other stimuli are defined as incorrect (−). Typically, the child is permitted to continue responding until the concept is learned. Learning is demonstrated when the subject chooses the correct stimulus on a specific number of consecutive trials, called the *criterion number*. The measure of the child's learning is the number of trials needed to reach this criterion performance level. This measure is therefore called *trials-to-criterion*.

An important characteristic of concept-learning tasks is that they usually involve several dimensions. In the previous example, shape (square or circle) was a dimension, and so was

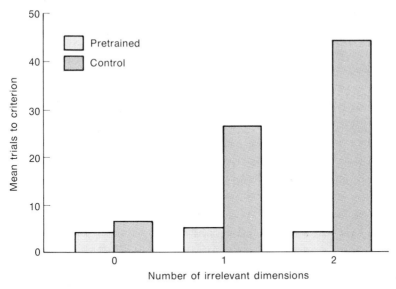

FIGURE 8.5
Mean number of trials-to-criterion as a function of the number of irrelevant dimensions represented in the stimuli. (Data from Tighe & Tighe, 1969. In Harold W. Stevenson. *Children's learning.* New York: Appleton-Century-Crofts, 1972. Copyright © 1972, p. 270. Reprinted by permission of Prentice-Hall, Inc., Englewood Cliffs, New Jersey.)

color (black or white). The shape dimension was important for solving the problem, so it is *relevant*. The color dimension, however, was not involved in the solution and is an *irrelevant* dimension. As the number of irrelevant dimensions increases, the difficulty of the problem also usually increases. However, Tighe and Tighe (1969) have demonstrated that this is not always the case. These researchers first taught one group of children to discriminate between different dimensions by making a series of "same-different" judgments (pretrained group). A second group of children received no pretraining (control group). Both groups of children were then tested on concept-learning problems involving zero, one, or two irrelevant dimensions. Greater numbers of irrelevant dimensions made the problem more difficult (more trials to criterion) for the control subjects, but children who had learned the difference between the dimensions performed well, regardless of the number of irrelevant dimensions (Figure 8.5).

Matching

A third form of accuracy measure is concerned with the similarity of the child's response to a predetermined correct response. That is, the child's behavior is accurate if it matches the behavior that the experimenter has established as the standard. Often the dependent measure is expressed as the degree (or percent) of accuracy displayed by the subject.

To illustrate, children's accuracy of imitation was studied as a function of different types of feedback (Vasta, 1976). The task involved copying patterns on a pegboard to match the patterns presented by a model. On each trial, the child was given feedback regarding his or her accuracy. One group received no feedback (nf); a second group was told only when it was right (r); a third group was told only when it was wrong (w); a fourth group was given feedback on every trial (r + w); and a fifth group received a corrective modeling procedure in which inaccurate responses were corrected (cm). The results of these groups over eight trial blocks (six trials per block) are presented in Figure 8.6. The accuracy of all groups increased over the series of blocks, but different forms of feedback resulted in different levels of matching.

Complexity

Not all tasks are designed to have right and wrong responses. Sometimes the nature of the response can vary along several dimensions, all of which are in a sense correct. Yet the nature of the behavior may provide important information to the experimenter regarding various psychological processes. In this section, we shall consider two such dimensions.

Naive-Sophisticated

Some research paradigms involve responses that can be very simple or that may reflect a considerably higher level of cognitive sophistication. This dimension is often defined by the

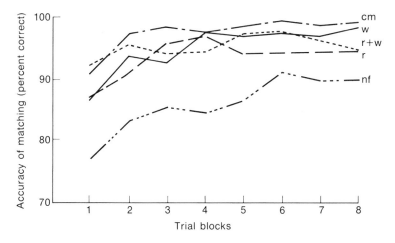

FIGURE 8.6
Accuracy of pattern imitation under each feedback condition: no feedback
(nf), right (r), wrong (w), right and wrong (r + w), and corrective modeling
(cm). (From R. Vasta. Feedback and fidelity: Effects of contingent
consequences on accuracy of imitation. *Journal of Experimental Child
Psychology*, 1976, **21**, 98–108. Copyright © 1976 by Academic Press, Inc.
Reprinted by permission.)

increasing abilities of children at older ages. Responses typically produced by eight-year-olds may be considered naive if
produced by ten-year-olds, but sophisticated if produced by
five-year-olds.

An example of this form of measure is illustrated by
"grouping" or *free-classification* studies. In such investigations,
children are presented with a collection of objects and instructed to arrange them in groups. Typically, the set of objects
vary along a number of dimensions, thereby providing the
child with the opportunity to construct very simple groupings
or more complex ones. In one study, two-year-old, three-year-
old, and four-year-old children were given thirty-two
cardboard figures of different sizes, shapes, and colors (Denney,
1972). Each subject was told: "What I want you to do is put
these things in different groups. Put the things that are alike or
the things that go together into groups." Six different types of
responses, ranging from simple to sophisticated, are illustrated

Design

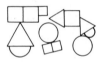

Design with similarity

Incomplete similarity on one dimension

Incomplete similarity on two dimensions

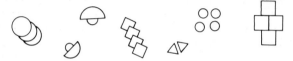

Complete similarity on one dimension

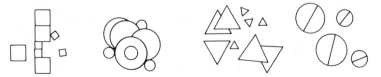

Complete similarity on two dimensions

FIGURE 8.7
Examples of different types of grouping responses. (From N. W. Denney. Free classification in preschool children. *Child Development,* 1972, **43,** 1161–1170. Copyright © 1972 The Society for Research in Child Development, Inc., by permission.)

TABLE 8.2
Frequencies of Different Types of Responses

Type of Response	Age 2	3	4
Design	3	2	1
Design with similarity	3	9	3
Incomplete similarity on one dimension	4	3	1
Incomplete similarity on two dimensions	9	7	5
Similarity on one dimension	1	8	12
Similarity on two dimensions	1	5	11

Source: N. W. Denney. Free classification in preschool children. *Child Development*, 1972, **43**, 1161–1170. Copyright © 1972 by The Society for Research in Child Development, Inc.

in Figure 8.7. The number of children producing these responses at various ages is presented in Table 8.2. Note how the complexity of the designs seems to be generally related to the age of the subject, demonstrating greater cognitive sophistication with increasing age.

Research involving children's language development often measures the sophistication of the verbal behavior under study. For example, in a well-known longitudinal study, the language development of three children was studied over a period of several years (Brown, Cazden, and Bellugi, 1969). One measure of interest was the increasing length of each child's utterances in terms of morphemes, or simple units of meaning. The data are presented in Figure 8.8, and they show that the complexity of the child's verbal behavior increases rapidly during this age-period. (This study is discussed again in Chapter 10).

Repetitive-Variable

A second dimension of complexity involves the variability of the response. Does the response always take the same form, or does it change as it occurs? This measure sometimes indicates the degree to which the child's behavior is flexible rather than stereotyped.

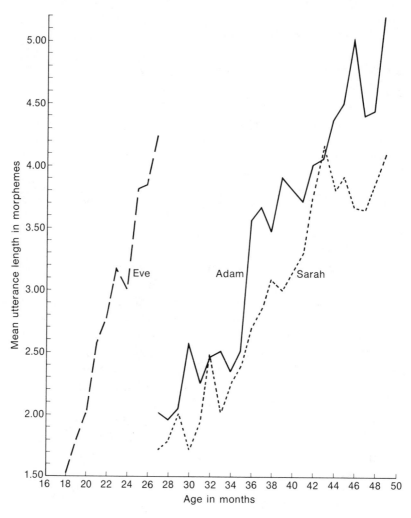

FIGURE 8.8
Mean length of utterance with increasing age for three children. (From C. B.
Cazden. The acquisition of noun and verb inflections. *Child Development*,
1968, **39**, 433–448. Copyright © 1968 The Society for Research in Child
Development, Inc., by permission.)

A relevant investigation concerns the amount of diversity
that children exhibit in their blockbuilding (Goetz and Baer,
1973). These researchers attempted to increase the variety of
forms that children used in their block constructions by re-

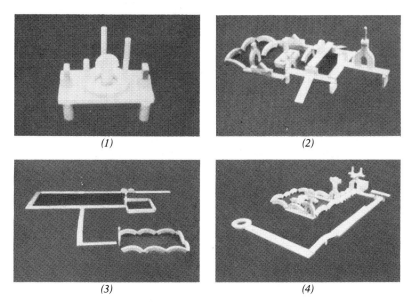

FIGURE 8.9
Block constructions by a preschool child under different conditions of
reinforcement: (1) baseline, (2) reinforcement for different forms, (3)
reinforcement for same forms, and (4) reinforcement for different forms.
(Courtesy Elizabeth M. Goetz.)

warding them for either repetitive or diverse forms. An A-B-C-B
time-series design was used, during which subjects were
praised either for using the same forms repeatedly ("How
nice—another tower!"), or for using different forms ("That's
nice—it's different!"). The responses made by one child under
each condition are presented in Figure 8.9. Note the repetitive
nature of the third construction and the more variable nature
of the second and fourth constructions. If we assume, in this
situation, that diversity reflects greater creativity, the variable
constructions would probably be considered the more creative.

Choice

Another important measure of behavior concerns neither
accuracy nor complexity but rather which response the child
will choose to perform. Most often this measure is used when
studying questions of *preference*. For example, will a child

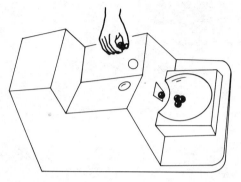

FIGURE 8.10
Apparatus used to measure hole preference for
marble-dropping game. (From J. L. Gewirtz
and D. M. Baer. Deprivation and satiation of
social reinforcers as drive conditions. *Journal
of Abnormal and Social Psychology*, 1958, **57,**
165–172. Copyright © 1958 by the American
Psychological Association. Reprinted by
permission.)

select a masculine- or feminine-stereotyped activity at play
(Barkley, Ullman, Otto, and Brecht, (1977)? Will a child choose
to spend more time looking at a word that has positive associations or one that has negative associations (Nunnally,
Duchnowski, and Parker, 1965)? Preference for producing a
particular response frequently results from the consequences of
such behavior. For this reason, choice measures are often used
to study the effects of various response-consequences.

   The factors affecting a particular response-consequence
were examined in a study by Gewirtz and Baer (1958). These
researchers hypothesized that the value of social approval
would be increased if children were deprived of this stimulation for a period of time, and it would be decreased if they had
just received a good deal of it. To test this idea, children in one
experimental condition were left alone in a waiting room for
twenty minutes before engaging in the experimental task (deprivation group). Children in a second condition began by
engaging in a simple drawing activity, for which the experi-

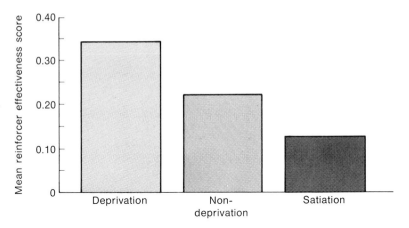

FIGURE 8.11
Effectiveness of social reinforcement in changing three groups of children's hole preferences for marble-dropping game. (From J. L. Gewirtz and D. M. Baer. Deprivation and satiation of social reinforcers as drive conditions. *Journal of Abnormal and Social Psychology*, 1958, **57**, 165–172. Copyright © 1958 by the American Psychological Association. Reprinted by permission.)

menter presented frequent social approval (satiation group). The remaining children did not experience either manipulation, but began the task immediately (nondeprivation group). The task involved the apparatus presented in Figure 8.10. Subjects were provided with a bowl of marbles and were instructed to drop them one at a time in either of the holes in the apparatus. Responses to one of the holes were followed by social approval from the experimenter ("fine" or "good"); no consequences followed responses to the other hole. The measure of interest was defined as the increase in preference for a particular hole as a result of the social approval (called the *reinforcer effectiveness score*). As can be seen in Figure 8.11, the effectiveness of social approval followed the researchers' predictions, with deprivation increasing its effectiveness and satiation decreasing its effectiveness.

Choice measures are also used to study *probability learning* problems (Weir, 1967). Often, an apparatus similar to the one in Figure 8.12 is used, which provides several similar response

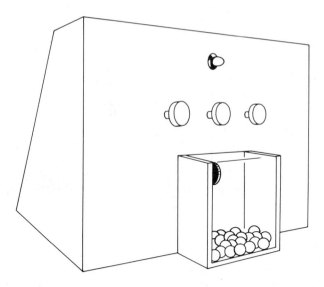

FIGURE 8.12
Apparatus used in probability-learning tasks. (From M. W.
Weir. Children's behavior in probabilistic tasks. Reprinted
by permission from *The Young Child: Reviews of Research*,
vol. 1, edited by Willard W. Hartup and Nancy L.
Smothergill, p. 137. Copyright © 1967 National Association
for the Education of Young Children, 1834 Connecticut
Avenue, N.W., Washington, D.C. 20009, by permission.)

buttons or levers. The child is instructed that each time the
light goes on, pushing one of the buttons will produce a reward
(for example, a piece of candy will drop out into a container).
The child's objective is to produce as many rewards as possible. Usually the experiment is designed in such a way that
each of the buttons has a different probability of producing a
reward on each trial. It is impossible, therefore, for the child to
select a strategy that will *always* produce a reward. But certain
strategies can be more effective than others. For example, if the
probability of reward by the three buttons is 0 percent, 66
percent, 33 percent, the most effective strategy would be for
the child to push the middle button *on every trial.* In this way,
the child would receive a reward, on the average, for two out of
every three trials. It is interesting that younger children and
adolescents perform most efficiently on such tasks—that is,

they choose the response that maximizes payoff. Middle-level children spread their responses among the alternatives, which proves to be the less-effective approach (Weir, 1964).

Additional Complex Measures

Many additional dependent measures involve relationships between a child's response and other factors. We shall describe two more measures which do not fit neatly into our previous categories.

Nature of Errors

At times, researchers can learn as much from the types of errors a child makes as from the correct responses he produces. Errors are often useful for indicating, not simply whether the child obtained the correct answer, but what sort of strategy or process was involved in the task. A study by Dirks and Neisser (1977) illustrates the value of this measure. The task involved testing memory for objects presented in three-dimensional scenes. Children were permitted to view a scene for thirty seconds. The scene was then changed by either (a) adding objects, (b) deleting objects, or (c) moving objects around. The scene was then shown to the subjects once again, and they were instructed to identify the changes that had occurred. A greater number of correct responses was given when items were added than for either of the other two conditions (Figure 8.13a). However, the number of false responses (errors) provided a very different pattern of results (Figure 8.13b). These data illustrate how different measures can often generate very different sorts of psychological information.

Sociometric Scores

Finally, we shall consider a dependent measure that is used to indicate a child's relationship to other children. This

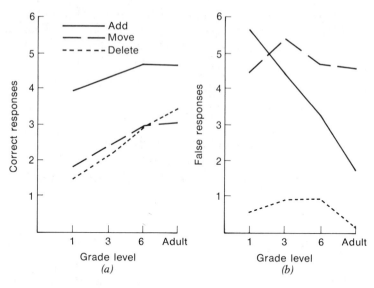

FIGURE 8.13

Mean number of correct responses (*a*) and false reports (*b*) for different ages and types of stimulus change. (From J. Dirks and U. Neisser. Memory for objects in real scenes: The development of recognition and recall. *Journal of Experimental Child Psychology*, 1977, **23**, 315–328. Copyright © 1977 by Academic Press, Inc. Reprinted by permission.)

relationship is assessed by having other children in the classroom answer questions regarding their opinion of or interaction with the subject. For example, each child in the class might be asked the question, "How much do you like to play with _____? Very much? A little? Or not at all?" The ratings of a particular subject by all other classmates could then be combined to produce a *sociometric* score, indicating some aspect of the child's popularity or influence in the class. Measures of sociometric status are often used when attempting to change the behavior of socially withdrawn or isolate children. For example, Oden and Asher (1977) investigated three techniques for improving the social skills of isolate third- and fourth-graders. Sociometric pretest measures were taken first, which indicated that these children were not regarded highly by their peers. Each subject was then given either (a) practice and verbal instructions on making friends (coaching condition), (b) practice in interacting with another child, but without the verbal instructions (peer pairing), or (c) a control condition. One measure of interest involved the changes in the children's sociometric ratings by their classmates. The group receiving coaching procedures showed more improvement than either of the other groups.

Conclusion

It should be apparent from this chapter and Chapter 7 that many aspects of children's behavior are of interest to the researcher. The relationships between various measures of behavior and the independent variables that produce the behavior offer an extremely rich source of scientific inquiry and speculation. And the ever-increasing amount and complexity of this information constantly generates new and important questions for study. Our understanding of the child continues to be limited perhaps only by our resourcefulness in finding methods to answer these many questions.

By now the reader should have a reasonably good idea of the many ways an investigator can set up a research experiment, and the reader should be able to begin evaluating actual published research reports. One useful exercise would be to select an issue of a research journal (discussed in Chapter 12) and, for each report presented, to determine the general type of research (Chapter 3), the basic research design (Chapters 4, 5, and 6), and the types of dependent measures involved (Chapters 7 and 8).

References

Barkley, R. A., Ullman, D. G., Otto, L., and Brecht, J. M. The effects of sex typing and sex appropriateness of modeled behavior on children's imitation. *Child Development*, 1977, **48**, 721–725.

Brown, A. L., and Murphy, M. D. Reconstruction of arbitrary versus logical sequences by preschool children. *Journal of Experimental Child Psychology*, 1975, **20**, 307–326.

Brown, R., Cazden, C. B., and Bellugi, U. The child's grammar from I to III. In J. P. Hill (ed.), *Minnesota Symposium on Child Psychology*, Vol. 2. Minneapolis: University of Minnesota Press, 1969.

Denney, N. W. Free classification in preschool children. *Child Development*, 1972, **43**, 1161–1170.

Dirks, J., and Neisser, U. Memory for objects in real scenes: The development of recognition and recall. *Journal of Experimental Child Psychology*, 1977, **23**, 315–328.

Gewirtz, J. L., and Baer, D. M. Deprivation and satiation of social reinforcers as drive conditions. *Journal of Abnormal and Social Psychology*, 1958, **57**, 165–172.

Goetz, E. M., and Baer, D. M. Social control of form diversity and the emergence of new forms in children's blockbuilding. *Journal of Applied Behavior Analysis*, 1973, **6**, 209–217.

Hale, G. A., and Piper, R. A. Developmental trends in children's incidental learning: Some critical stimulus differences. *Developmental Psychology*, 1973, **8**, 327–335.

Nunnally, J. C., Duchnowski, A. J., and Parker, R. K. Association of neutral objects with rewards: Effects on verbal evaluation, reward expectancy, and selective attention. *Journal of Personality and Social Psychology*, 1965, **1**, 270–274.

Oden, S., and Asher, S. R. Coaching children in social skills for friendship making. *Child Development*, 1977, **48**, 495–506.

Tighe, L. S., and Tighe, T. J. Transfer from perceptual pretraining as a function of number of task dimensions. *Journal of Experimental Child Psychology*, 1969, **8**, 494–502.

Vasta, R. Feedback and fidelity: Effects of contingent consequences on accuracy of imitation. *Journal of Experimental Child Psychology*, 1976, **21**, 98–108.

Weir, M. W. Developmental changes in problem-solving strategies. *Psychological Review*, 1964, **71**, 473–490.

Weir, M. W. Children's behavior in probabilistic tasks. In W. W. Hartup and N. L. Smothergill (eds.), *The young child: Reviews of research*. Washington: National Association for the Education of Young Children, 1967.

9   Techniques
with Infants

The period of infancy, usually regarded as lasting from birth to eighteen months of age, is considered by most psychologists to be an extremely important phase of human development. Much that occurs during this period sets the stage for later learning and occasionally has long-range effects. Yet, in many ways, our knowledge of the processes occurring in infancy lags considerably behind that of other development periods. The most important reason for this lag is that our research methods in this area have only recently begun to overcome some of the major problems presented by the study of infants.

In the last chapter, we reviewed a number of the more popular techniques used to study older children. Many of these techniques involved relatively complex behavior on the part of the child—naming, describing, manipulating, following directions, and so on. The infant, however, possesses fewer of these response capabilities. For example, most of the human newborn's behaviors are simple reflexes, which are gradually replaced by only very rudimentary motor behaviors. The infant cannot yet use language, so it cannot tell us what it is doing, feeling, seeing, or thinking, nor can it even follow our instructions. The challenge, then, is to devise methods of studying the infant that can effectively utilize this very minimal repertoire of responses. We shall see that this is being achieved with remarkable success.

The purpose of this chapter is not to present all of the many techniques that have been adapted to studying the infant. Rather, we hope simply to illustrate the often imaginative ways in which psychologists have taken very basic processes and principles and used them to reveal surprisingly complex information about the child.

Many of these techniques are based on conditioning and learning principles. It will not be necessary to have previous knowledge of these principles to understand our coverage of these techniques. But the interested student might find a review of these procedures useful before pursuing this area in more depth (see, for example, Reese and Lipsitt, 1970; Whitehurst and Vasta, 1977).

Habituation-Dishabituation

One important area of interest is assessing infants' sensory capabilities. How well can they see? What range of sound differences can they detect? Can they distinguish one odor from another? A particularly effective technique for investigating many such questions is the *habituation-dishabituation* paradigm.

Habituation is actually a very simple form of human learning involving reflexes (inborn responses that can reliably be produced by presenting a specific stimulus). Human infants display many reflexes, such as sucking when a nipple is presented to the mouth, startling when a loud noise is presented, grasping when an object is placed in its palm, and so on. *Habituation* occurs when a reflex is elicited repeatedly over a short period of time and begins to decrease in intensity (magnitude). For example, if we clap our hands loudly near a newborn, a marked startling response probably will occur. But if we continue to clap our hands every twenty seconds, the magnitude of the startle gradually will decrease, and the response may even disappear entirely. This process represents a rather primitive form of learning, yet it has become extremely useful for investigating infants' sensory discrimination abilities.

An example of the use of this technique can be found in studies of visual acuity (Friedman, 1972; Friedman, Bruno, and Vietze, 1974). These researchers were interested in determining how well infants can perceive visual detail at very early ages. To study this question, the visual fixation response was employed. It has been shown that when a new stimulus is presented in an infant's visual field, the infant will look at it for a period of time. If the stimulus is repeatedly removed and re-presented, however, the infant's fixation on it will gradually decrease. This decline is the *habituation* process. If a different stimulus is then presented, the magnitude of the infant's response may quickly return to its original high level. This recovery is termed *dishabituation,* and it indicates that the infant has recognized that the new stimulus is, in fact, different from the previous one. The presence or absence of the dishabituation process can be used to determine whether infants perceive the new stimulus as the same or different—that is, whether they can differentiate the new stimulus from the original stimulus.

In these studies, infants' abilities to discriminate between checkered patterns of different complexity was examined. For example, some subjects were presented with a simple, two by two, black and white pattern for repeated sixty-second trials. At the end of each trial, the stimulus was removed for five seconds and then presented again for sixty seconds. At first, infants spent almost the entire minute looking at the stimulus, but gradually their viewing time on each trial decreased. When this habituation of the response was clearly demonstrated, a stimulus of different complexity was substituted for the original pattern. The results for two pattens are illustrated in Figure 9.1. Different results were found for male and female newborns. Males did not display dishabituation to the new stimulus—that is, they responded to it as if it were the original stimulus, which suggests that they could not discriminate between the two patterns. The females, however, showed a clear recovery of the looking response, indicating their superior visual acuity during the first days of life.

The habituation paradigm is particularly valuable to researchers of infant behavior because it requires only minimal response capabilities. Simple reflexes are sufficient to demon-

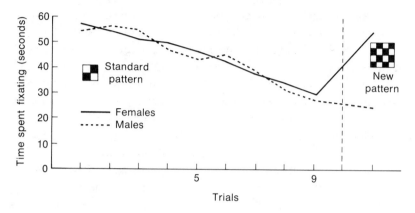

FIGURE 9.1
Mean fixation time for each sixty-second pattern presentation for nine
habituation trials and shift to new pattern. Only females show dishabituation
to the novel stimulus. (Adapted from Friedman, Bruno, and Vietze, 1974.)

strate complex sensory abilities. In addition, the technique has
been shown to work in a variety of sensory modalities, including auditory abilities (Bridger, 1961; Bartoshuk, 1962) and olfactory sensitivity (Engen and Lipsitt, 1965).

Satiation

Another method for investigating infant sensory abilities
uses a different response system. Rather than using reflex responses, the satiation paradigm involves the more voluntary
operant response. These responses differ from reflexes because
they are influenced by their consequences. Operant responses
that are followed by satisfying or rewarding outcomes (reinforcement) tend to reoccur, whereas operant responses followed by aversive consequences (punishment) are less likely to
reoccur.

One method of studying infant operant responses involves
the use of contingent reinforcement. Simply stated, this procedure provides that the rate of the infant's response will determine the rate or amount of the reinforcing consequence. For

example, it is possible to arrange such a relationship between an infant's sucking responses and the presentation of sounds by using a pressure-sensitive nipple mechanically attached to audio-production equipment. The higher the rate of infant sucking, the greater the number of sounds that are produced (also see the section on Conjugate Reinforcement later in this chapter).

Satiation refers to the phenomenon where the value of certain reinforcing outcomes will decrease if they are presented repeatedly. If the infant's sucking produces a particular sound that the infant finds interesting, the rate of sucking will be maintained. After a while, however, the value of this consequence may decline, and the rate of sucking will begin to decrease. If a novel sound is now substituted for the original, and the infant can perceive it as something new, the rate of sucking will often increase once again. As with dishabituation, the presence or absence of this increase informs the researcher whether the infant can detect the change in stimuli.

Trehub (1973) has used this paradigm to study infants' auditory abilities. First, a contingent reinforcement relationship was established between sucking and the presentation of a particular one-syllable sound (pa, ta, or a). The sucking responses that produced the sound gradually decreased over a five-minute period, but when the sound was changed (pi, ti, or i), the rate of sucking recovered to a high level (Figure 9.2). Thus, the infants obviously were capable of detecting the difference in vowel sounds.

The satiation paradigm has been used primarily in the study of auditory abilities (Eimas, Siqueland, Jusczyk, and Vigorito, 1971; Morse, 1972). It has been used to a lesser degree to investigate infants' visual abilities (Milewski and Siqueland, 1975).

Visual Fixation

The techniques described thus far can be used to measure the child's ability to discriminate among various stimuli. A related question concerns the infant's preferences for these

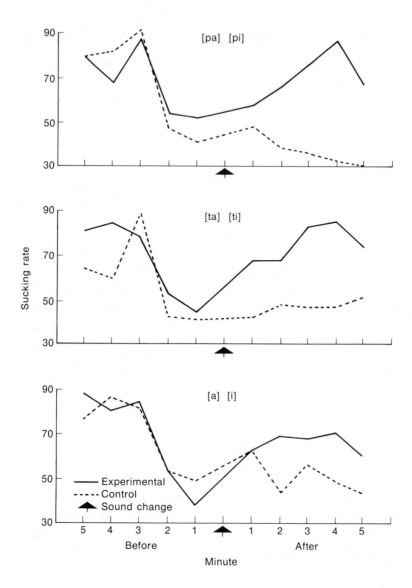

FIGURE 9.2
Amount of sucking to produce sounds, five minutes before and after change to a new sound. Increase in sucking at sound change indicates discrimination of novel stimulus. Sound change occurred only for experimental group. (From S. Trehub. Infants' sensitivity to vowel and tonal contrasts. *Developmental Psychology*, 1973, **9**, 91–96. Copyright © 1973 by the American Psychological Association. Reprinted by permission.)

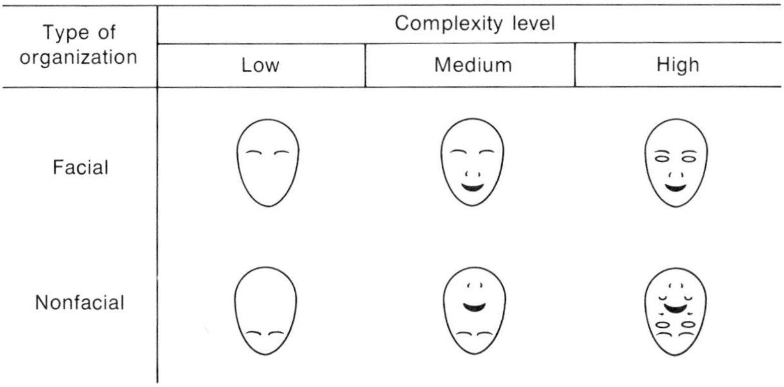

Type of organization	Complexity level		
	Low	Medium	High
Facial			
Nonfacial			

FIGURE 9.3
Stimulus patterns representing three levels of complexity and two types of organization. (From R. A. Haaf and C. J. Brown. Infants' response to facelike patterns: Developmental changes between 10 and 15 weeks of age. *Journal of Experimental Child Psychology*, 1976, **22**, 155–160. Copyright © 1976 by Academic Press, Inc. Reprinted by permission.)

stimuli. For example, there is reason to suspect that children's preferences for the complexity of visual stimuli change as they grow older (Munsinger, Kessen, and Kessen, 1964; Thomas, 1966). Do infants also seek out particular levels of visual complexity and avoid stimuli that are too simple or too complex?

A rather straightforward method of assessing infants' visual preferences involves observing the relative amounts of time the subject fixates on various stimuli. A clear demonstration of the effectiveness of this measure has been reported by Haaf and Brown (1976). Two independent variables were examined in this study: (1) complexity of the stimuli, and (2) whether they were organized as facial or nonfacial patterns. Six schematic patterns were used, representing three levels of complexity and two types of organization (Figure 9.3).

The infants lay on their backs, where they could view the stimuli presented above them. At the same time, the experimenter observed and recorded the amount of time their eyes actually fixated on each stimulus while it was in view. The patterns were presented in pairs, using various combinations of

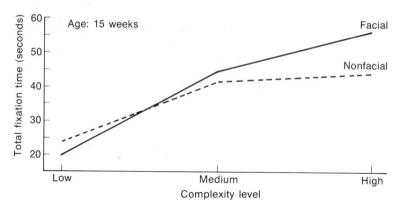

FIGURE 9.4

Fixation times for infants for three complexity levels of facial and nonfacial stimuli. (From R. A. Haaf and Brown. Infants' response to facelike patterns: Developmental changes between 10 and 15 weeks of age. *Journal of Experimental Child Psychology*, 1976, **22**, 155–160. Copyright © 1976 by Academic Press, Inc. Reprinted by permission.)

the stimuli. The average amount of time the fifteen-week-old infants looked at each of the six patterns is shown in Figure 9.4.

The results indicate an "interaction" between the two variables (see Chapter 5). That is, the infants preferred stimuli of increasingly greater complexity when a facial pattern was presented. Preference for complexity was only moderate, however, when nonfacial stimuli were presented.

Familiarization-Novelty

One of the more exciting infant research paradigms to be developed in recent years is the familiarization-novelty method (Fagan, 1970, 1972, 1974). The purpose of this paradigm is to study visual discrimination abilities, but it also permitted, for the first time, the investigation of early memory capabilities.

The method combines the visual fixation procedures with the habituation-dishabituation procedures. Two identical visual stimuli are presented simultaneously to familiarize the subject with these figures. The amount of visual fixation de-

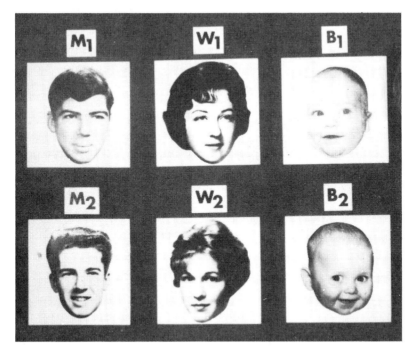

FIGURE 9.5
Two sets of stimulus patterns used in infant memory task. (From J. F. Fagan.
Infants' delayed recognition memory and forgetting. *Journal of Experimental
Child Psychology*, 1973, **16**, 424–450. Copyright © 1973 by Academic Press,
Inc. Reprinted by permission.)

voted to each stimulus is noted. At the end of the initial viewing period, one of the familiar figures is replaced with a new
one, first on the left side, then on the right. If the subject
spends more time looking at the new stimulus, it is clear that
the infant can perceive it as novel. In addition, familiar stimuli
can be compared with novel stimuli hours or even days after
initial viewing to determine whether infants continue to remember them.

An example of the latter method has been reported by
Fagan (1973). The visual stimuli were the six photos of human
faces shown in Figure 9.5. Infants first were exposed to a pair of
identical stimuli (for example, W_1-W_1) for two minutes. Test
sessions consisted of two ten-second presentations of one of the

original stimuli with each of the other stimuli in that set (for example, W_1-M_1 and B_1-W_1). Testing that occurred immediately after the familiarization period may be considered simple discrimination tests. But, as the time before testing is increased, the issue becomes one of infants' memory abilities. In this investigation, six-month-old subjects displayed evidence of facial recognition in tests conducted at periods of three hours, twenty-four hours, forty-eight hours, one week, and two weeks!

This paradigm is particularly impressive in that it permits exploration of a complex cognitive ability (memory) without requiring a complex response from the infant. The next method also illustrates a clever procedure for examining cognitive abilities in newborns.

Interruption

Perhaps the best example of a simple measure that reveals complex information is the *response-interruption* paradigm. It is impossible to know what (if anything) an infant is thinking, or precisely how it views and understands the world. But we can begin to probe infants' thought processes by determining what kinds of things disconcert or surprise the infant. One such procedure measures the amount of behavior interruption caused by a stimulus or event. If an infant is engaging in a repetitive behavior, such as sucking, the behavior will cease if the infant suddenly views an unexpected event.

Bower (1965) used this method to study infants' development of "perceptual unity." That is, when and how do infants determine that certain visual stimuli represent a single unit (an object)? One characteristic that infants may use to identify an object is the continuation, or unbroken line, of the outline of the object. For example, in Figure 9.6 the visual stimulus in A_1 has a discontinuous outline, whereas the stimulus in B_1 has a more uniformly continuous outline.

Infants were placed in a crib where visual stimuli were presented above them. A nipple was placed in the subject's mouth, and rate of sucking was recorded. If children use the

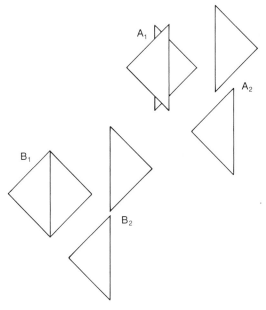

FIGURE 9.6
Stimuli used to study "perceptual unity." Pattern B_1 has a more continuous outline than pattern A_1. Older infants show greater surprise when stimuli transform to B_2 than to A_2. (From T. G. R. Bower. The determinants of perceptual unity in infancy. *Psychonomic Science*, 1965, **3**, 323–324. Copyright © 1965 Psychonomic Society, Inc. by permission.)

continuation characteristic to identify objects, then stimulus B_1 would be perceived as more of a unit than stimulus A_1. To test this hypothesis, infants should show more surprise to the separation of the B_1 triangles. Using a filmed presentation, the infants witnessed the stimuli transform to A_2 and B_2. The measure of cognitive surprise was the degree to which their sucking was interrupted during the transformation. Younger infants failed to show more surprise at the separation of the continuous stimulus, suggesting that they do not yet use this perceptual characteristic to determine unity. However, beyond six months of age, this event evokes considerable behavior interruption.

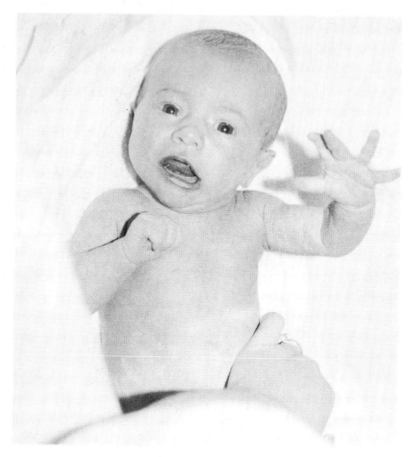

FIGURE 9.7
Infants' response capabilities are much more limited than those of older children, making the development of effective research techniques a challenging task. (Photograph by Larry Wallnau.)

Additional Techniques

There are far too many specific infant-study techniques to enumerate all of them. The ones described thus far were selected in part because of their imaginative nature and also because they can be applied to a relatively large number of different experimental questions. Several additional well-known techniques will be described briefly in this section. In most cases, they are less adaptable to many issues of study.

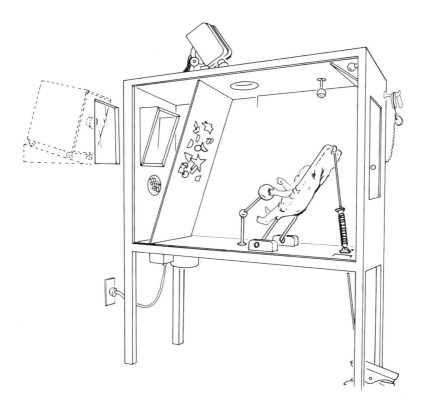

FIGURE 9.8
A device used to study conjugate reinforcement in infants. As the infant
manipulates the sphere, the brightness and clarity of the visual stimulus
increase. (From H. L. Rheingold et al. Method for studying exploratory
behavior in infants. *Science*, 1962, **136,** 1054–1055. Copyright © 1962 by the
American Association for the Advancement of Science, by permission.)

Conjugate Reinforcement

A special case of contingent reinforcement can be arranged whereby the rate of the child's behavior affects not only
the *rate* of the reinforcement but its *quality* as well. An example
of such a conjugate reinforcement contingency is illustrated in
Figure 9.8. The response involves manipulation of the sphere.
The consequence is the presentation of the visual stimulus. As
the child's rate of responding increases, the rate of the reinforcer, as well as its brightness and clarity, also increase

FIGURE 9.9
The visual cliff apparatus used to study early depth perception. (Photograph
by William Vandivert. Reprinted by permission from William Vandivert
and Scientific American.)

(Rheingold, Stanley, and Cooley, 1962). This procedure is used
primarily to examine simple operant learning, including the
identification of effective reinforcers (Fagen and Rovee, 1976;
McKirdy and Rovee, 1978).

Visual Cliff

The area of perceptual development has generated a
number of interesting investigatory techniques. A famous device for studying infants' depth perception is the visual cliff

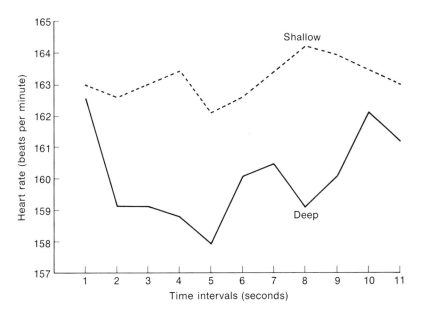

FIGURE 9.10

Heartbeat rate responses of two-month-old infants on the visual cliff apparatus. A decrease indicates attention rather than fear. (From J.J. Campos. Heartrate: A sensitive tool for the study of emotional development in the infant. Copyright © 1976 by Lawrence-Erlbaum Associates, Inc. Reprinted by permission.)

apparatus (Gibson and Walk, 1960). Infants are placed on a glass surface, which covers areas of different depths (Figure 9.9). Almost all six-month-old infants studied in this way venture freely over the "shallow" end but refrain from crossing the "deep" side. This suggests that they perceive the different depths of the two areas and show fear of the deeper one. This apparatus has also been used in conjunction with more physiological (rather than behavioral) measures when testing younger infants. Two-month-old infants also show evidence of perceiving the different depths, as measured by a change in their rate of heart-beat when placed over each side (Campos and Langer, 1971). However, their heart-beat rates *decrease* when they are placed over the deeper side, suggesting an attentional response rather than fear, which apparently develops later (Figure 9.10).

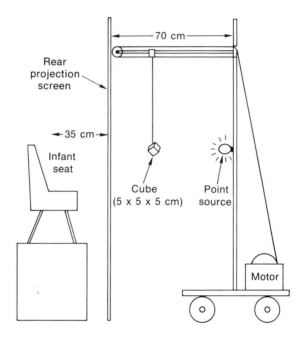

FIGURE 9.11
Shadow-casting apparatus used to study an infant's
response to impending collision. (From W. Ball and E.
Tronick. Infant responses to impending collision: optical
and real. *Science*, 1971, **171,** 818–820. Copyright © 1971
by the American Association for the Advancement of
Science, by permission.)

Impending Collision

Another method of investigating infants' depth perception
is to determine whether they perceive an object as quickly
approaching. A device used to test this question is a shadow-
casting apparatus (Ball and Tronick, 1971). Infants are seated
before a screen, upon which a shadow is projected from the
rear. The shadow is produced by a light shining on a hanging
object (Figure 9.11). When the light source is moved closer to
the object, the shadow of the object expands, thereby creating
the illusion that the object is approaching. The response under
study involves an avoidance of the impending collision with

the object. This includes such behaviors as moving the head back and putting the arms up in front of the face. Infants as young as two months of age give evidence of avoidance in this situation, indicating a very early perception of depth using these visual cues.

Playtest

Most research involving infants' preferences has been devoted to the visual modality. This has been true partly because the infant's response to visual stimuli is very easy to measure (visual fixation). It is possible to study preferences for auditory stimuli as well, if older infants are used. Friedlander (1968) has devised an apparatus known as *Playtest* for this purpose. The device consists of two levers mounted on the side of the subject's playpen. The levers are connected to two separate sound sources. The child can produce the auditory stimuli by depressing one lever. By programming various combinations of sound stimuli, Friedlander has shown that one-year-old infants prefer the sound of their mother's voice to music and to a stranger's voice. The apparatus has also been used to demonstrate the relationship between infants' listening preferences and spontaneous vocalizations. Specifically, infants vocalized less when hearing their preferred parent's voice (Barrett-Goldfarb and Whitehurst, 1973).

Conclusion

The study of infancy holds great promise for our ultimate understanding of human development. It also provides an important test of our ability to generate new and effective methods of investigation. Several of the more prominent methods have been discussed; many others have not. A number of excellent sources of additional in-depth discussions of this area include Bower, 1974, 1977; Gordon, 1975; and Lipsitt, 1976.

Of course, the techniques presented in this chapter, as well as in Chapters 7 and 8, have dealt principally with laboratory methods. Much research involving infants, however, is conducted in more natural settings. In Chapter 10 we shall consider the techniques and methods used in these settings.

References

Ball, W., and Tronick, E. Infant responses to impending collision: optical and real. *Science*, 1971, **171**, 818–820.

Barrett-Goldfarb, M. S., and Whitehurst, G. J. Infant vocalization as a function of parental voice selection. *Developmental Psychology*, 1973, **8**, 273–276.

Bartoshuk, A. K. Response decrement with repeated elicitation of human neonatal cardiac acceleration to sound. *Journal of Comparative and Physiological Psychology*, 1962, **55**, 9–13.

Bower, T. G. R. The determinants of perceptual unity in infancy. *Psychonomic Science*, 1965, **3**, 323–324.

Bower, T. G. R. *Development in infancy*. San Francisco: W. H. Freeman and Company, 1974.

Bower, T. G. R. *A primer of infant development*. San Francisco: W. H. Freeman and Company, 1977.

Bridger, W. H. Sensory habituation and discrimination in the human neonate. *American Journal of Psychiatry*, 1961, **117**, 991–996.

Campos, J. J., and Langer, A. The visual cliff: Discriminative cardiac orienting responses with retinal size held constant. *Psychophysiology*, 1971, **8**, 264–265.

Eimas, P. D., Siqueland, E. R., Jusczyk, P., and Vigorito, J. Speech perception in infants. *Science*, 1971, **171**, 303–306.

Engen, T., and Lipsitt, L. P. Decrement and recovery of responses to olfactory stimuli in the human neonate. *Journal of Comparative and Physiological Psychology*, 1965, **59**, 312–316.

Fagan, J. F. Memory in the infant. *Journal of Experimental Child Psychology*, 1970, **9**, 217–226.

Fagan, J. F. Infants' recognition memory for faces. *Journal of Experimental Child Psychology*, 1972, **14**, 453–476.

Fagan, J. F. Infants' delayed recognition memory and forgetting. *Journal of Experimental Child Psychology*, 1973, **16**, 424–450.

Fagan, J. F. Infant recognition memory: The effects of length of familiarization and type of discrimination task. *Child Development*, 1974, **45**, 351–356.

Fagen, J. W., and Rovee, C. K. Effects of quantitative shifts in a visual reinforcer on the instrumental response of infants. *Journal of Experimental Child Psychology*, 1976, **21**, 349–360.

Friedlander, B. Z. The effect of speaker identity, voice inflection, vocabulary, and message redundancy on infant's selection of vocal reinforcement. *Journal of Experimental Child Psychology, 1968*, **6**, 443–459.

Friedman, S. Habituation and recovery of visual response in the alert human newborn. *Journal of Experimental Child Psychology*, 1972, **13**, 339–349.

Friedman, S., Bruno, L. A., and Vietze, P. Newborn habituation to visual stimuli: A sex difference in novelty detection. *Journal of Experimental Child Psychology*, 1974, **18**, 242–251.

Gibson, E. J., and Walk, R. D. The "visual cliff." *Scientific American*, 1960, **202**, 64–71.

Gordon, I. J. *The infant experience.* Columbus, Ohio: Charles E. Merrill, 1975.

Haaf, R. A., and Brown, C. J. Infants' response to facelike patterns: Developmental changes between 10 and 15 weeks of age. *Journal of Experimental Child Psychology*, 1976, **22**, 155–160.

Lipsitt, L. P. (ed.). *Developmental psychobiology.* Hillsdale, N.J.: Lawrence Erlbaum, 1976.

McKirdy, L. S., and Rovee, C. K. The efficacy of auditory and visual conjugate reinforcers in infant conditioning. *Journal of Experimental Child Psychology*, 1978, **25**, 80–89.

Milewski, A. E., and Siqueland, E. R. Discrimination of color and pattern novelty in one-month human infants. *Journal of Experimental Child Psychology*, 1975, **19**, 122–136.

Morse, P. A. The discrimination of speech and nonspeech stimuli in early infancy. *Journal of Experimental Child Psychology*, 1972, **3**, 477–492.

Munsinger, H., Kessen, W., and Kessen, M. L. Age and uncertainty: Developmental variation in preference for variability. *Journal of Experimental Child Psychology*, 1964, **1**, 1–15.

Reese, H. W., and Lipsitt, L. P. *Experimental child psychology.* New York: Academic Press, 1970.

Rheingold, H. L., Stanley, W. C., and Cooley, J. A. Method for studying exploratory behavior in infants. *Science,* 1962, **136,** 1054–1055.

Thomas, H. Preferences for random shapes: Ages six through nineteen years. *Child Development,* 1966, **37,** 843–859.

Trehub, S. Infants' sensitivity to vowel and tonal contrasts. *Developmental Psychology,* 1973, **9,** 91–96.

Whitehurst, G. J., and Vasta, R. *Child behavior.* Boston: Houghton Mifflin, 1977.

10 Observational Methods

In earlier chapters we examined some of the various types of dependent measures that are of interest to child psychologists. As noted earlier, the measures may be assessed either in a tightly controlled laboratory setting or in more natural settings. Most of the methods discussed in this chapter are used in natural settings, such as the home or classroom. These settings present special demands for the researcher and require a number of unique methodological considerations.

Use of Observational Techniques

When research is conducted in the laboratory, the actual collection of data is often performed by automated devices. Electronic counters may keep track of the number of times a child pushes a button, or the pattern of an infant's visual scanning might be recorded by a special eye-movement camera. Even when such instrumentation is not used, laboratory research often involves very objective, quantifiable measures. For example, we might assess a child's concept-learning by counting the number of errors made before reaching the solution, or we might assess the child's moral development by

159

noting which of several situations the child selects as most fair. In either case, the degree of precision and accuracy of these methods is usually quite high and is of no particular issue to the investigator.

When we move our research interests to field settings, however, data collection methods usually do not involve such direct and objective procedures. More often, human observers are employed to identify and record the data of interest. There are three principal reasons for this. First, it is often impractical and expensive to make specialized laboratory equipment sufficiently portable for such use. Second, there are still many behaviors and events that cannot be measured only with automated devices—a smile, a question, an imitative gesture, and so on. It is true that we can use filming or taping devices to record these events, but it is still necessary for human observers to *identify the occurrence* of such behaviors. Finally, the use of human observers in naturalistic settings often results from the kinds of questions or issues under investigation. For example, by using observers the psychologist can frequently study the child without interfering with the usual course of events. This is useful if the investigator is interested in learning what normally occurs in the child's world, rather than under more artificial laboratory conditions. Such information may be valuable in its own right, or it may provide the basis for later research in a more rigorous laboratory situation.

For these reasons, observational methods play an important part in the scientific study of children. But, as we have suggested, these procedures do not necessarily possess the objectivity of most laboratory procedures, and certain safeguards are required to ensure a high degree of accuracy. Later in the chapter we shall examine the most important types of observational methods. But before doing so, let us consider some of the issues common to all these methods.

Any investigator planning to use observational techniques must begin by answering four general questions. The answers to these questions will vary dramatically depending on the observational method to be used and, more importantly, on the questions under study.

1. *What will be observed?* This apparently straightforward question can often have a complex answer. The psychologist undoubtedly will wish to observe certain behaviors of the child, but exactly which ones and precisely how to define them may not always be so obvious. If the psychologist, for example, is interested in observing attachment behaviors in an infant, the list of specific behaviors could be potentially quite long—for example, approaching the mother, visual pursuit, clinging, smiling, and so on. It is also necessary to define the behaviors of interest in a manner that makes them easy to identify. The behavior of "vocalizations directed to the mother" may require considerable detailed explanation when observers actually try to separate these responses from other infant vocalizations occurring in the mother's presence. In addition to observing behaviors of the child, the investigator may wish to record other events as well. The behavior of others in the child's environment, for example, as well as the entire range of physical and social events occurring during the period of observation, are also frequently data of interest. Clearly, many decisions of this type must be made before observations can begin.

2. *When will the observations be made?* Related to this question is the issue of how long or how many observations will be involved. This answer again depends on the nature of the research topic, but there is a very important issue here that is common to all observational studies. Because the observations will occur only for a limited period of time (even if the period is very long), it is crucial that the data be *representative* of the information of interest to the researcher. For example, a single one-hour observation of the child in the home may provide a very distorted sample of the child's typical behavior, especially if it happens to occur during an unusual circumstance, such as during illness or during a holiday. Likewise, observations made during a particular part of the day may not accurately reflect the total story, as with children who are attentive in the classroom during morning hours but get restless and disruptive later in the day. And if there is any suspicion that the observation procedures are initially reactive (see Chapter 2), it may be necessary to continue the procedure until such effects stabilize or disappear. These common sources of bias in observational studies should be considered very carefully in advance by the researcher.

3. *Which observational method will be used?* There are many possible answers to this question, and yet there is really just one. The investigator should use the method that most efficiently and accurately provides the information of interest. We shall not discuss the various methods in detail at this point, because they will be examined shortly. But it is important to note that the experimenter should be aware of the different types of procedures available, including their strengths and weaknesses, so that the most appropriate method may be selected.

4. *How will the accuracy of the observations be verified?* In many ways, this is the most important question of all, because if the experimenter cannot be confident that the observations represent what actually occurred, the data are of no scientific value. The major problem that can arise here is that the observer may not accurately record the behaviors or events being observed. This may occur for a variety of reasons, such as insufficient observational skills, prior expectations of what will occur, poorly defined behaviors, and so on. The usual safeguard for dealing with these possibilities is the use of several observers, each recording the behaviors independently. The observations then are compared, and their similarity or *reliability* is determined mathematically. If they are sufficiently similar, the researcher typically assumes that they also are reasonably accurate. There are a variety of such reliability procedures, and again the researcher should understand them before selecting the one most appropriate for the data. This topic and related issues will be considered in more detail later in the chapter.

The four general questions we have just discussed are only the minimum number that must be considered before observational research begins. Many other specific decisions could be discussed as well, including the nature and training of the observers, the use of film or tape equipment to provide a permanent record of the observed events, the openness of the observational procedures versus the use of hidden or unobtrusive observers, and so on. In each case, the answers to these questions should be considered in advance, keeping in mind the unique characteristics or requirements of the research problem.

Types of Observations

The many different types of procedures that have been used to observe children can be arranged in various ways. In this section, the methods will be grouped primarily according to the nature of the actual observation procedures used in the research. Within these groupings, we shall then consider the nature of the situation under observation. Using this classification scheme, four principal methods of observational study can be identified.

Informal Observations

The first group of methods is presented principally for historical interest. These methods involve no formal observation system and thus are open to considerable bias and distortion. Typically, these reports have consisted of simple descriptions of several aspects of the child's activities, and the observations were usually made at relatively unsystematic intervals.

The earliest of these accounts are the now-famous *baby biographies*, some of which were produced as early as the eighteenth century (Tiedemann, 1787; Preyer, 1888–1889). Among the most famous of these reports is Charles Darwin's description of the behavior and development of his son "Doddy," published in 1877. Darwin recorded many detailed characteristics of the infant, including initial reflex reactions, early evidence of fear or anger, and even more sophisticated behavior sequences presumed to display reasoning or moral development. More recently, under the supervision of psychologist Joseph Church, three mothers kept detailed diaries of one of their newborns for the first two years of life. Church gave the mothers some broad guidelines as to what to observe, but he generally suggested that the record ". . . whatever they found amusing, surprising, or puzzling" (Church, 1966, p. vii). These biographies were then revised and published by Church in 1966 as a book entitled *Three Babies*.

Baby biographies often present a fascinating look at the actual world of the child, but they also suffer from important

FIGURE 10.1
Informal, naturalistic observations often serve to alert researchers to
interesting aspects of human behavior, but such observations lack the rigor
necessary for scientific analysis. (Photograph by Emilio A. Mercado.)

scientific shortcomings. One of the more obvious shortcomings
is the selective, or unsystematic, nature of most of the observations. Whatever the observer found interesting or important at
any given moment may have been included, while many other
important behaviors and events went unrecorded.

A related observational procedure is found in the early
writings of Swiss psychologist Jean Piaget. Piaget also initially kept informal diaries of his children, but later his observations evolved into what he called the *clinical method*. This
procedure involved presenting the child with various specific

situations or problems and noting their reactions. By repeating these presentations as the child grew older, Piaget observed and recorded developmental changes that occurred in different aspects of the child's behavior. This approach is clearly more scientific, because some structure was introduced into the observation situation. However, Piaget's actual observational system remained only informal note-taking, so his own personal reactions or interpretations cannot be verified.

Data obtained by such informal observations cannot be considered of direct scientific value, because they lack the necessary guarantees of objectivity. Such casual observations, however, often can alert the investigator to potentially important phenomena, which later may be examined under more rigorous conditions. This form of observation, then, does have some merit.

Indirect Observations

Some psychologists have chosen to study children's behavior by methods that do not involve direct observations. Instead, the researchers have attempted to obtain the information of interest from other sources.

The most common method of indirect observation involves the *parental interview* technique. In this procedure, the experimenter asks the child's parents to recount specific behaviors or events regarding their child. The actual interview procedure may be quite controlled and structured, or it may permit the parent to elaborate on particular situations in a less-structured manner. A well-known example of this procedure was reported in a study by Schaffer and Emerson (1964). These investigators interviewed thirty-seven mothers of newborns at regular intervals over a period of about one year. The questions were concerned primarily with situations where the mother and infant were in physical contact, and they included information regarding both the child's behavior and the mother's. From the mothers' descriptions, the researchers drew a number of conclusions, the most important being that infants can be reasonably divided into "cuddlers" and "non-cuddlers."

The parental interview procedure also presents some important problems for a rigorous scientific analysis. Much of the parents' report may involve subjective judgments or interpretations, which can easily be inaccurate. Such distortions may be unintentional, but they also may involve some tendency to present information that seems to "please" the researcher or avoids making the parent appear incompetent or negligent.

A less frequently used indirect method is the *retrospective report* (see Chapter 4). Here the adolescent or adult subject is asked to recall the events and circumstances of childhood. Researchers using this approach often attempt to relate these retrospective data to current characteristics of the subject, such as certain personality traits or attitudes. For example, Schaefer (1965) has developed a questionnaire known as the Child's Report of Parental Behavior Inventory, in which the subject answers a series of specific questions regarding his or her parent-child relationship. Burger (1975) used this instrument to show, for instance, that college females' early relationships with their mothers appear to be related to their current levels of femininity and socialization.

Again, this approach is subject to considerable distortion, particularly when many years have passed. What one remembers may be partly a result of his or her current situation and attitudes—often exactly the variables that the retrospective data are supposed to predict. Neither form of indirect observation permits verification of the accuracy of the data, making them generally less-preferred than direct techniques. As we shall see, even direct, highly quantified methods are subject to bias; it is likely, then, that indirect methods are even less reliable in this regard.

Stream of Behavior

The third general approach to observation can be described loosely as the collection of *streams of behavior*. In this approach, samples of the child's activities, and often the concurrent behavior of others in the environment, are recorded as completely as possible over a limited, but systematic, period of time. For example, an experimenter may observe a child each day for one hour, recording as precisely as possible what the child does and experiences during that interval. These samples of behavior and events are analyzed and coded into meaningful units, which then become the data of interest.

There are several important advantages of this procedure over the informal methods discussed previously. The observations are not done casually or randomly, but have a planned basis to them. They may only comprise a small fraction of the child's total behaviors, but they are designed to be a representative sample of those behaviors. In addition, although the data are initially recorded without any systematic observation plan, the information later is reobserved using specific rules and procedures. This procedure permits the data to be analyzed by independent observers so that checks are made on the reliability of the findings.

One of the earliest major projects using this method was conducted by Barker and Wright during the 1940s and 1950s (Barker and Wright, 1951, 1955). These researchers were of the *ecological* tradition (see Chapter 3), and they were interested in studying the typical daily activities of children in a small Kansas town they called "Midwest." A team of observers was trained to make detailed recordings of every behavior in which a particular child engaged; the observers also recorded many aspects of the immediate environment. These massive collections of observations, known as *specimen records*, were then coded by the researchers into two basic units. *Behavior episodes* described a cohesive behavioral interaction by the child, and *behavior settings* described the environmental circumstances in which the episodes occurred. These units then were analyzed into larger sequences, and conclusions regarding typical child-behavior and experiences were drawn.

The study of children's language development has used the stream of behavior approach perhaps more than any other area of research. This research often has been developmental in nature, with data being collected on the same subjects over months or years. The earliest research data were diaries of the experimenters' own children; extensive note-taking procedures were used (e.g., Leopold, 1939–1949). Recent studies typically have involved periodic visits to the children's homes, with data collection being performed by audio or audio-video tape recorders. When the speech sample, known as a *corpus* in this research, has been transcribed, it is analyzed and coded into whatever units the researchers deem most suitable.

The most famous project of this sort was conducted by a Harvard research team headed by Roger Brown (Brown and Bellugi, 1964; Brown, Cazden, and Bellugi, 1969). These investigators collected speech samples of three children, Adam, Eve, and Sarah, over a two-year period (see Chapter 8). The observer visited the child's home every other week and recorded at least two hours of the spontaneous speech of both the mother and child. These speech samples were then coded into primitive types of grammar used by the children. From these observations and those of other investigators (e.g., Braine, 1963; Bloom, 1970), a great deal has been learned about the typical course of children's language acquisition.

Many stream-of-behavior studies, such as those just described, have been concerned principally with observations in unstructured, naturalistic settings. Some researchers using this approach, however, have conducted such observations under more controlled conditions. For example, Shatz and Gelman (1973) were interested in examining the complexity of speech that four-year-olds use when interacting with their mothers or with a two-year-old child. The experimenters arranged a somewhat structured situation, in which the child was given a particular toy and asked to talk about its workings with the mother or the two-year-old. The dialogue between the two subjects was recorded and later examined to identify the kinds of statements or language constructions that were used.

If conducted appropriately, observations collected in streams of behavior, which are later analyzed and verified, can be an important scientific tool. The method compromises some experimental rigor, because the precise determinants of a behavior cannot always be clearly and convincingly identified. But, because these procedures retain so much of the natural flavor of the child's interactions, they provide excellent sources of naturalistic information and ideas for future research.

Formal Observations

The fourth and most important group of observational methods are those that include systematic observing and recording procedures. Such methods not only consider the time and duration of the observation period, but also the precise behaviors to be observed and the procedures used to record them. In addition, reliability estimations are typically provided by multiple, independent observers. Three principal methods of formal observations have been used by child psychologists.

The first involves the use of *rating scales.* Observers usually are required to score the subject on a number of dimensions, or continuous scales, for which the end-points are described. For example, on the dimension

Timid   Outgoing
            1 2 3 4 5 6 7

the observers might have to indicate their impression of the child's social interactions by circling the appropriate number.

A study using this type of procedure was conducted by a research group interested in mother-infant interactions (Stern, Caldwell, Hersher, Lipton, and Richmond, 1969). The observation setting was a clinic, where the pediatrician interviewed the mother and child. Several observers sat behind one-way screens and recorded characteristics of both the mother and the infant. The scales used to observe the personality characteristics of both mother and child included such dimensions as dominance-permissiveness, emotionality-placidity, and changeability-sameness. More specific behavior scales included vocal expressions of affection and self-confidence for the mother and alertness and irritability for the infant. Scores on these various scales were then intercorrelated (compared in all possible combinations) to try to identify important relationships between characteristics of the mother and characteristics of the infant. One shortcoming of this particular research was that observer reliability was not assessed. Such verification procedures can easily be included in the rating-scale method, however, simply by having observers work independently and compare their data. But one problem with this method is that it still requires considerable subjective judgment on the part of the observer. Therefore, reliability between observers often is not very high.

Another method of formal observation involves counting the *frequency of occurrence* of the behaviors of interest during the observation period. The crucial feature of this procedure is that these behaviors, called *target behaviors*, must be defined with enough detail so that observers working independently can reliably identify their occurrence or nonoccurrence. Because of the greater emphasis on objective definitions, this method usually results in better reliability scores than the rating-scales approch and is much more popular among child-development researchers.

A study by Rogers-Warren and Baer (1976) illustrates this procedure. These researchers examined several classroom procedures that might increase *sharing* and *praising* among preschool children. These two classes of behavior were defined as follows (p. 337):

> *Sharing.* Two classes of sharing, verbal sharing and nonverbal sharing, were recorded. Verbal sharing included any verbalization by a subject to a peer in which the subject (1) invited a peer to join in a particular activity, or (2) verbally accepted the invitation of a peer to join in a particular activity, or (3) offered to share materials with a peer, or (4) verbally accepted peer's offer to share materials, or (5) offered to trade materials with a peer. Nonverbal sharing was recorded when one subject passed or handed a material to a second subject, if both subjects had touched the material within 5 sec., or when two or more subjects simultaneously used the same material (e.g., colored on the same sheet of paper at the same time).

> *Praising.* Praising was defined as any verbalization by a subject to a peer in which the subject indicated approval, liking, or admiration for the peer or any aspect of the peer's art work. There are essentially four forms of praise: (1) "I like . . ." and a general object (e.g., "I like your *picture*"); (2) "I like . . ." and a specific object or quality (e.g., "I like *the way you used the color blue*"); (3) direct general praise (e.g., "neat picture" or "pretty"); and (4) direct specific praise (e.g., "Nice *dogs*" or "That's a pretty *house* you made").

A structured situation was created, during which the children sat on the floor around a large piece of paper and worked with art materials. Ten minutes of observation in this setting were carried out each day, four times per week. Observations were made by three observers seated within viewing range of the subjects. All instances of sharing or praising were recorded; also recorded were to which child the behavior was directed and what materials were shared. Two of the observers divided their observations among different children; the third observer recorded behaviors of children from both groups to provide multiple observations on each child. These multiple observations then were compared to assess the accuracy of the observation procedures. We shall discuss reliability calculations shortly, but it is worth noting that, using these procedures, the reliability among observers was quite high.

The frequency-of-occurrence method is most useful when the observation periods are short in duration, as in the present study. When longer periods are used, however, reliability estimates tend to decrease. To deal with this problem, it is necessary to break the observation period into smaller recording intervals as described in the next technique.

Certainly the most advanced and frequently used observation procedures are a group called *interval-sampling* or *time-sampling* techniques. The idea behind this approach is that it is much easier for observers to agree on the occurrence or nonoccurrence of a behavior during a short period than during a longer one. Observation intervals, therefore, are divided into very small units—often only ten seconds. At the end of this interval, the observers record whether the target behaviors have occurred and then immediately begin the next interval. Twenty minutes of such observation could thus produce over one hundred intervals on which independent observers could compare their recordings. Again, target behaviors typically are well-defined to increase the likelihood of accurate observations.

To illustrate this technique, we shall consider an applied research project conducted with a single child (Thomas, Nielsen, Kuypers, and Becker, 1968). The subject was a six-year-old male who exhibited many disruptive behaviors in the classroom. The focus of the study was to improve the teacher's methods of dealing with the student. However, we shall consider only the observational procedures used to assess the child's behavior. Nine categories of disruptive behavior were defined as follows (p. 295):

Gross Motor Getting out of seat, standing up, walking around, running, hopping, skipping, jumping, rocking chair, moving chair, arm flailing, and rocking body without moving chair.

Kneeling Kneeling in seat, sitting on feet, and lying across desk.

Aggression Hitting, pushing, shoving, pinching, slapping, poking, or using an object to strike another child.

Disturbing Others Grabbing objects or work belonging to another child, knocking objects off a neighbor's desk, destroying property of other children, throwing objects.

Talking Conversing with other children, calling teacher, blurting out answers or questions, and singing.

Vocalization Crying, screaming, coughing, sneezing, whistling, and other non-verbal vocalizations. (Both Talking and Verbalization were rated only when the observer could hear the response as well as see its source.)

Noise Rattling or tearing papers, throwing books or other objects onto his desk, tapping feet, clapping, slamming desk top, tapping desk with objects, kicking or scooting desk or chair. (Again, the action had to be seen and the noise heard.)

Orienting While seated, the child turns head or both head and body toward another person, shows objects to others, looks at others. (Looking less than four seconds was not rated unless accompanied by a turn of more than 90° from desk. Whenever an Orienting response overlapped two time intervals, and could not be rated in the first, it was rated in the second interval if the total response met the time criterion.)

Other Tasks The child is doing things other than those prescribed by teacher which are not included in the above categories (e.g., playing with objects, looking at the floor, untying his shoe laces, wringing his hands, ignoring questions).

It is important to note the detail included in the definition of each behavior. For example, if the child whispered something into the ear of another student, the observers would have known not to record it as Talking or Vocalization (because they could not *hear* it).

Observation periods were twenty minutes long, and recording was done at ten-second intervals. All observers initially were trained in the use of this scoring system to ensure familiarity and skill with the observation procedures. They also used special scoring-sheets and stop-watches to increase the precision of their recordings. A typical scoring-sheet from this study might look like the one in Figure 10.2.

The first observations are scored in the upper left box, representing the first recording interval of the first minute of observation. At the end of ten seconds of observation, the observer would simply circle the appropriate code for each of the nine target behaviors that had been displayed by the child during the previous ten seconds. Only one circle is drawn, even if the same behavior occurred several times. The observer then would observe for ten more seconds and record those observations in the next box to the right, and so on until twenty minutes of data were collected.

There are several alternatives to the recording procedures used in this study. For example, some investigators prefer to have behaviors scored only if they occur for the *entire* ten-second interval, and others only score the behavior if it is occurring at the *end* of the interval. Also, sometimes the actual recording is separated from the observation of the child (for example, *observe* for ten seconds, *record the data* for five seconds).

As we mentioned earlier, the time-sampling technique is the most advanced and most sophisticated of our current observational approaches. It objectifies human observational procedures more than any other method; more importantly, it permits an accurate assessment of the reliability of the observations. Because this particular technique is so important, we shall devote the next sections to a brief discussion of reliability procedures and some remaining sources of observational bias.

Observation intervals (seconds)

Minutes	0-10	11-20	21-30	31-40	41-50	51-60
1	G K A D T V N O OT	G K A D T V N O OT	G K A D T V N O OT	G K A D T V N O OT	G K A D T V N O OT	G K A D T V N O OT
2	G K A D T V N O OT	G K A D T V N O OT	G K A D T V N O OT	G K A D T V N O OT	G K A D T V N O OT	G K A D T V N O OT
3	G K A D T V N O OT	G K A D T V N O OT	G K A D T V N O OT	G K A D T V N O OT	G K A D T V N O OT	G K A D T V N O OT
4	G K A D T V N O OT	G K A D T V N O OT	G K A D T V N O OT	G K A D T V N O OT	G K A D T V N O OT	G K A D T V N O OT
5	G K A D T V N O OT	G K A D T V N O OT	G K A D T V N O OT	G K A D T V N O OT	G K A D T V N O OT	G K A D T V N O OT
6	G K A D T V N O OT	G K A D T V N O OT	G K A D T V N O OT	G K A D T V N O OT	G K A D T V N O OT	G K A D T V N O OT
7	G K A D T V N O OT	G K A D T V N O OT	G K A D T V N O OT	G K A D T V N O OT	G K A D T V N O OT	G K A D T V N O OT
8	G K A D T V N O OT	G K A D T V N O OT	G K A D T V N O OT	G K A D T V N O OT	G K A D T V N O OT	G K A D T V N O OT
9	G K A D T V N O OT	G K A D T V N O OT	G K A D T V N O OT	G K A D T V N O OT	G K A D T V N O OT	G K A D T V N O OT
10	G K A D T V N O OT	G K A D T V N O OT	G K A D T V N O OT	G K A D T V N O OT	G K A D T V N O OT	G K A D T V N O OT
11	G K A D T V N O OT	G K A D T V N O OT	G K A D T V N O OT	G K A D T V N O OT	G K A D T V N O OT	G K A D T V N O OT
12	G K A D T V N O OT	G K A D T V N O OT	G K A D T V N O OT	G K A D T V N O OT	G K A D T V N O OT	G K A D T V N O OT
13	G K A D T V N O OT	G K A D T V N O OT	G K A D T V N O OT	G K A D T V N O OT	G K A D T V N O OT	G K A D T V N O OT
14	G K A D T V N O OT	G K A D T V N O OT	G K A D T V N O OT	G K A D T V N O OT	G K A D T V N O OT	G K A D T V N O OT
15	G K A D T V N O OT	G K A D T V N O OT	G K A D T V N O OT	G K A D T V N O OT	G K A D T V N O OT	G K A D T V N O OT
16	G K A D T V N O OT	G K A D T V N O OT	G K A D T V N O OT	G K A D T V N O OT	G K A D T V N O OT	G K A D T V N O OT
17	G K A D T V N O OT	G K A D T V N O OT	G K A D T V N O OT	G K A D T V N O OT	G K A D T V N O OT	G K A D T V N O OT
18	G K A D T V N O OT	G K A D T V N O OT	G K A D T V N O OT	G K A D T V N O OT	G K A D T V N O OT	G K A D T V N O OT
19	G K A D T V N O OT	G K A D T V N O OT	G K A D T V N O OT	G K A D T V N O OT	G K A D T V N O OT	G K A D T V N O OT
20	G K A D T V N O OT	G K A D T V N O OT	G K A D T V N O OT	G K A D T V N O OT	G K A D T V N O OT	G K A D T V N O OT

G—Gross motor	D—Disturbing	N—Noise
K—Kneeling	T—Talking	O—Orienting
A—Aggression	V—Vocalization	OT—Other tasks

FIGURE 10.2

A typical observation code sheet. Observations are conducted every ten seconds over the twenty-minute period. The observer circles the appropriate code for behaviors that occur during each observation interval.

Estimating Observer Reliability

There are so many ways to calculate the amount of agreement between observers that some question exists as to which methods are best (Kent and Foster, 1977). We will describe the most frequently used procedures, which are generally accepted by most researchers.

When collecting data for reliability purposes, it is necessary to have two observers each observe the same subject at the same time. These multiple observations do not have to cover the entire observation period, however. For example, if a child is being observed each day for sixty minutes by the principal observer, the second observer (reliability assessor) commonly observes the child for only ten to fifteen minutes of that time. In some research, reliability observations are not even conducted during every observation session, although it is usually considered desirable for them to be.

The data from the reliability assessor are then compared with that same portion of the principal observer's data. Two decisions must be made at this point (Hartmann, 1977). The first concerns the *unit* of reliability. In the Thomas et al. (1968) study, for example, we might wish to calculate the amount of observer agreement separately for *each* of the nine categories of behavior, or we might combine the data over all nine categories and simply calculate the amount of agreement on the occurrence of *any* disruptive behavior. The general rule here is that reliability should be calculated separately for those units about which the investigator plans to draw conclusions. If the experimenter is concerned with the specific effects of the treatment on a particular behavior (for example, orienting), the first procedure should be used. But if the interest is only in the treatment effects on disruptive behavior, then the second procedure would be acceptable. The second decision concerns the *time-span* of the reliability. For example, the amount of interobserver reliability could be calculated for each session, or for a group of sessions, or simply for all the sessions combined. Again, the general rule is that reliability data should not be combined over time-periods that are to be discussed separately. For example, if the first five observation sessions involved no treatment procedures (baseline), and the next ten sessions involved an intervention procedure (treatment), the data should be combined, at most, over the first five and next ten sessions. In fact, in the case of both *units* and *time-span*, the less the data are combined, the more accurate the reliability estimates are likely to be.

The mathematical procedures used by most researchers to assess interobserver agreement are rather straightforward. The best approach is to compare the total number of agreements of the *occurrence* of a behavior with the total number of agreements plus disagreements of its occurrence. To illustrate, consider the data in Figure 10.3, a scoring-sheet similar to that of Thomas et al. (1968). In *(a)* are the data of four minutes of observation by the principal observer; in *(b)* are the data of the reliability assessor for the same four minutes. We shall consider only the reliability of the observations of noise (N).

For each ten-second interval, there are four possible combinations of scoring: (A) both observers record that the behavior occurred, (B) only the principal observer records its occurrence, (C) only the reliability assessor records its occurrence, and (D) neither observer records the occurrence of the behavior. The formula usually used to calculate reliability is:

$$\text{Reliability} = \frac{A}{A + B + C} \times 100$$

This formula can be restated as the percent of the time that the observers agreed, *when at least one of them recorded the occurrence of the behavior.* None of the intervals in which both agreed that the behavior did not occur (D) are included in the calculations.

In the data of Figure 10.3, the reliability formula yields the following scores:*

$$\text{Reliability} = \frac{16}{16 + 1 + 1} \times 100 = 89\%$$

*The interested reader is encouraged to calculate the reliability from the data in Figure 10.3 to ensure that the procedures are understood. The reliability for the orienting (o) data should be 0.68. Reliability estimates for the two remaining behaviors can also be calculated and compared with the results obtained by others.

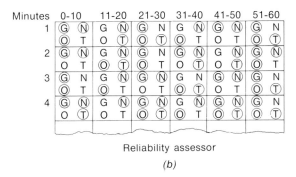

FIGURE 10.3
Four minutes of observation by an observer and a reliability asessor. Reliability is determined by comparing observations made by each observer in the same time-intervals.

Most investigators require a minimum reliability score of 80 percent before the data can be accepted with much confidence. Therefore, these observations would appear to be sufficiently consistent to accept the data.

This reliability procedure is only one of many acceptable methods. What is most important here is that *some* reliability procedure should always be included when using observational methods, to guarantee at least a minimum degree of confidence in the data.

Sources of Observational Bias

Despite the rigor of the time-sampling approach compared with other observational methods, some potential for distorted observations remains. Some of these problems can be dealt with rather easily, but others may prove considerably more difficult to eliminate.

The first source of bias involves the subjects of the observations and is termed *reactivity* (see Chapter 2). This means simply that the behavior of subjects sometimes changes when they know they are being observed. Two general solutions have been proposed to deal with this problem. It has been noted that the reactive effects of observations sometimes decrease after a period of time. Therefore, one solution involves simply continuing the observations over a long enough period for the behaviors to stabilize—presumably at their normal levels. Unfortunately, it is often difficult to be certain when and if this has occurred, making this solution less than foolproof. The second alternative is to employ unobtrusive or covert means of observation. Hidden cameras or one-way viewing mirrors are frequently used so that subjects are not aware of the data collection. This approach is more likely to eliminate reactivity, but it is not always a possible or practical solution in many settings.

A second source of bias involves the observers themselves. We have already discussed the value of objective procedures and reliability assessment as means of reducing observer distortion. But even very well-quantified procedures can result in biased observations under some circumstances. For example, some kinds of observational data seem to be particularly sensitive to *expectations* by the observers. That is, if the observers are led to believe that a child's behavior, for example, will become less disruptive, they are somewhat more likely to see the behavior in this fashion (Kent, O'Leary, Diament, and Dietz, 1974). A related problem involves *feedback* to the observers from the researchers. If the observers are led to believe that the experimenter is either pleased or disappointed with their findings, there is some tendency for the observers to produce data that are consistent with the experimenter's wishes (O'Leary,

(a)

(b)

(c)

FIGURE 10.4
Observational methods sometimes can have reactive effects if subjects are acutely aware of the observations (a). This problem can be solved by making the observer more unobtrusive (b) or by using a one-way glass (c).

Kent, and Kanowitz, 1975). Both of these problems can be solved if the observers are kept "blind" (unaware of the experimental predictions). Again, this is not always possible.

Another problem involving the observers is *knowledge of reliability assessment*. It has been shown that if an observer is aware that a second observer is assessing reliability, there is a greater tendency for their observations to be similar than if reliability is assessed unobtrusively (Taplin and Reid, 1973). This effect probably results from the observers being more attentive or alert in their observations when they know they are being checked. Obviously, the best way to solve this problem is to keep observers unaware of when reliability assessments are occurring.

Finally, a third source of bias is related to the experimenter's observation procedures. One such problem involves

TABLE 10.1
Observational Bias

Source	Solution
Subjects	
Reactivity	Extended observation period; unobtrusive measures
Observers	
Expectations	"Blind" observers
Feedback	Avoidance of evaluative comments
Knowledge of reliability assessment	Unobtrusive reliability checks
Experimenter	
Code complexity	Use of simple code; adequate training of observers
Inflated estimate of reliability	Use of appropriate reliability statistic

code complexity. If observers are required to use a scoring system involving many different types of behaviors or events, lower reliability estimates usually occur (Mash and McElwee, 1974). This can be partially eliminated by better training procedures, but it also should indicate to the experimenter that there are limits to human observer capabilities. Another possible bias involves the experimenter's selection of procedures for *reliability estimation.* As we suggested in the preceding section, there are many ways to calculate interobserver reliability, with some methods producing generally higher estimates of agreement than others (Kent and Foster, 1977). In selecting a reliability procedure, therefore, the investigator should take precautions against using a method that will imply more observer accuracy than probably occurred.

Whether the source of bias is the subject, the observer, or the experimenter, the resulting data will not reflect the true information of interest (see Table 10.1). Even worse, unless the experimenter is aware of such distortions, these biased data may be accepted as reasonable bases for drawing experimental conclusions. We can only wonder how frequently this situation may have occurred in the past.

Conclusion

We have seen that observational methods are necessary in the study of child development and probably will remain so for many years. The sophistication of these methods has increased dramatically since the early, informal observational techniques, and it continues to improve as research progresses. Nevertheless, there still exists a great deal of subjectivity in human observations, and we are not yet close to a method of human observation whose precision approaches that of modern instrumentation. It is crucial, therefore, that we remain alert to possible biases in conclusions drawn solely from observational data. Until recently, many sources of bias remained unknown, and it seems likely that there are others yet to be discovered.

References

Barker, R. G., and Wright, H. F. *One boy's day*. New York: Harper & Row, 1951.

Barker, R. G., and Wright, H. *Midwest and its children: The psychological ecology of an American town*. New York: Harper & Row, 1955.

Bloom, L. M. *Language development: Form and function in emerging grammars*. Cambridge, Mass.: M.I.T. Press, 1970.

Braine, M. D. S. The ontogeny of English phrase structure: The first phase. *Language*, 1963, **39**, 1–13.

Brown, R. W., and Bellugi, U. Three processes in the child's acquisition of syntax. *Harvard Educational Review*, 1964, **34**, 133–151.

Brown, R. W., Cazden, C., and Bellugi, U. The child's grammar from I to III. In J. P. Hill (ed.), *Minnesota Symposium on Child Psychology* (Vol. 2). Minneapolis: University of Minnesota Press, 1969.

Burger, G. Recalled parental behavior, sex roles, and socialization, *Journal of Clinical Psychology*, 1975, **31**, 292–298.

Church, J. (ed), *Three babies: Biographies of cognitive development*. New York: Random House, 1966.

Darwin, C. A biographical sketch of an infant. *Mind*, 1877, **11**, 286–294.

Hartmann, D. P. Considerations in the choice of interobserver reliability estimates. *Journal of Applied Behavior Analysis*, 1977, **10**, 103–116.

Kent, R. N., and Foster, S. L. Direct observational procedures: Methodological issues in naturalistic settings. In A. R. Ciminero, K. S. Calhoun, and H. E. Adams (eds.), *Handbook of behavioral assessment*. New York: John Wiley, 1977.

Kent, R. N., O'Leary, K. D., Diament, C., and Dietz, A. Expectation biases in observational evaluation of therapeutic change. *Journal of Consulting and Clinical Psychology*, 1974, **42**, 774–780.

Leopold, W. *Speech development of a bilingual child: A linguist's record* (Vols. 1–4). Evanston, Ill. Northwestern University Press, 1939–1949.

Mash, E. J., and McElwee, J. D. Situational effects on observer accuracy: Behavior predictability, prior experience, and complexity of coding categories. *Child Development*, 1974, **45**, 367–377.

O'Leary, K. D., Kent, R. N., and Kanowitz, J. Shaping data collection congruent with experimental hypotheses. *Journal of Applied Behavior Analysis*, 1975, **8**, 43–51.

Preyer, W. *Mind of the child*. Translated by H. W. Brown. New York: Appleton, 1888–1889.

Rogers-Warren, A., and Baer, D. M. Correspondence between saying and doing: Teaching children to share and praise. *Journal of Applied Behavior Analysis*, 1976, **9**, 335–354.

Schaefer, E. S. Children's report of parental behavior: An inventory. *Child Development*, 1965, **36**, 413–421.

Schaffer, H. R., and Emerson, P. E. Patterns of response to physical contact in early human development. *Journal of Child Psychology and Psychiatry*, 1964, **5**, 1–13.

Shatz, M., and Gelman, R. The development of communication skills: Modifications in the speech of young children as a function of listener. *Monographs of the Society for Research in Child Development*, 1973, **38**, No. 5.

Stern, G. G., Caldwell, B. M., Hersher, L., Lipton, E. L., and Richmond, J. B. A factor analytic study of the mother-infant dyad. *Child Development*, 1969, **40**, 163–181.

Taplin, P. S., and Reid, J. B. Effects of instructional set and experimenter influence on observer reliability. *Child Development*, 1973, **44**, 547–554.

Thomas, D. A., Nielsen, L. J., Kuypers, D. S., and Becker, W. C. Social reinforcement and remedial instruction in the elimination of a classroom behavior problem. *The Journal of Special Education,* 1968, **2,** 291–305.

Tiedemann, D. Observations on the mental development of a child. In W. Dennis (ed.), *Historical readings in developmental psychology.* New York: Appleton-Century-Crofts, 1972 (first published in German in 1787).

IV

Related
Issues

11 Ethical Considerations

Until now, we have approached the study of children from an objective, scientific point of view. The selection of research procedures or methods of investigation has been based primarily on their ease of administration and their ability to answer our research questions unambiguously. These considerations are of course crucial for drawing clear, scientific conclusions. Additional criteria, however, must be considered when human subjects are the focus of study. These criteria involve the legal, moral, and ethical aspects of our research. That is, in attempting to answer a particular experimental question regarding children, might our procedures inadvertently produce negative effects on our subjects or violate any of their individual rights or privileges?

Until recently, child psychologists did not have to confront these issues. In fact, a number of classic investigations by well-known psychologists were conducted using procedures that would now be considered highly questionable. John B. Watson, for example, demonstrated the conditionability of fear reactions by producing a phobia in eleven-month-old "Little Albert" (Watson and Raynor, 1920). Wayne Dennis and his wife investigated the role of social stimulation on child development by raising a pair of twins in virtual seclusion for twelve months (Dennis, 1941).

These investigators did not have evil or malicious intent. There simply were no prohibitions to these research practices, and the scientific spirit of the times apparently put greater emphasis on the value of the knowledge than the rights of the individuals involved. Today, the situation has changed dramatically, and ever-increasing attention is being drawn to the ethical considerations of research with children (Smith, 1967). For example, the *Society for Research in Child Development*, an organization of professional child researchers, has adopted an ethical code governing its members in their scientific investigations. This code is presented at the end of the chapter in Table 11.1.

The purpose of this chapter is to acquaint future researchers and consumers of psychological research with some of these issues. We shall review the major hazards and objectionable practices that may occur when studying children, as well as some safeguards that have been introduced to deal with them.

Physical or Psychological Harm

The foremost area of concern is that the research procedures may produce damaging effects on the subjects under study. Physical injury or pain certainly would be the clearest form of this problem. Psychologists interested in the variables affecting the development of motor skills, for example, might wish to investigate the effects on the infant of inadequate nutrition or long periods of restricted movement. These experimental manipulations obviously pose a threat to the child's well-being and could not be considered acceptable procedures. In many such cases, researchers conduct their investigations with lower animals and they simply assume that similar results might be found with humans. From a strictly scientific point of view, this practice is unfortunate because it provides only indirect information regarding the issue. But from an ethical viewpoint, it is a necessary alternative.

The question of psychological harm, in contrast, is much less clear. For example, what exactly constitutes a negative psychological effect? Certainly it would be easy to agree on many extreme cases, such as the case of a child who begins to lie and cheat after experimental exposure to a similarly deceitful adult model. But how do we evaluate research procedures that produce in the child such reactions as fear, embarrassment, or failure?

An investigator might be interested, for example, in studying the effects of success or failure in performing a task on a child's subsequent willingness to perform a similar activity. One straightforward method of addressing this problem would be, first, to expose one group of subjects to repeated success experiences on the task, and, second, to expose another group to repeated failures. These two experimental groups (along with any other control groups) could then be tested on the dependent measure of interest. The concern here, of course, is that some subjects in this study will leave the experimental session having been continually exposed to failure experiences, and perhaps they will feel such emotional reactions as frustration or humiliation.

It is possible to defend these procedures on the grounds that such emotional reactions often appear to vanish shortly after the study is concluded. One might argue, therefore, that they pose no long-term threat. Nevertheless, psychologists are increasingly of the opinion that procedures producing these reactions are undesirable, and they have begun substituting procedures that tend to minimize such effects.

One approach is to include a final procedure for all children which suggests that they have performed well. This might take the form of an additional easy task or simply verbal feedback that their performance was very good. In our example, the experimenter might have followed the dependent measure with several more trials of the original task on which all children would succeed.

An alternative way to avoid this problem would be to use a different research design. For example, instead of using the between-subjects approach just described, the psychologist might have had each child work on one task under success conditions and a second task under failure conditions. This within-subjects design, of course, would then require the use of several tasks as dependent measures for each child. This type of solution has been particularly useful in single-subject time-series research (see Chapter 6). Following the collection of baseline data, the introduction of the treatment procedures is often effective in changing the target behavior (for example, reducing classroom aggression). From an experimental point of view, it is then desirable to reinstate baseline conditions (reversal procedure) to demonstrate that the treatment was in fact responsible for the change in behavior. In some cases, however, it may be considered ethically improper to generate the problem behavior again, even for a brief period. An increasingly popular solution to this dilemma involves the substitution of a different experimental design—often a *multiple-baseline* approach. This method might involve introducing the treatment first in the classroom, then in the playground, and finally in the home. In this way, a functional relationship could be demonstrated between the treatment and the target behaviors (satisfying the scientist) without having to reinstate the problem once it was removed (satisfying the teachers and parents).

A final safeguard against possible psychological harm is a procedure called *debriefing*. In research with adults, psychologists are ethically bound to inform the subjects about the purpose of the research after the completion of the study. This debriefing process is particularly crucial when any sort of *deception* was involved—that is, when any aspect of the procedure was concealed from the subject, or when certain information was distorted intentionally. The use of debriefing procedures with children, however, is somewhat problematic. It is reasonable to use this procedure with older children, but debriefing a younger child can sometimes be worse than doing nothing. For example, admitting to children that you had deceived them might provide an inappropriate model, suggesting that lying is justifiable. Moreover, the child may become suspicious of adults in other situations. For such reasons, some psychologists suggest that intentional deception should never be used with younger children (Baumrind, 1977). Whether we take this approach, avoid debriefing entirely, or use some other form of feedback to the child, it is important for the researcher to remain aware of this problem.

Violation of Privacy

A second type of ethical problem concerns violations of personal privacy and confidentiality. When studying human subjects, the psychologist often must obtain personal information about the subject, sometimes using deceptive methods. These practices raise both ethical and legal questions regarding the rights of research subjects and the protection of their civil liberties.

The first important issue involves simply the willingness of the subject to participate in the investigation. It used to be relatively common for psychologists to gather information about unsuspecting subjects, perhaps by arranging a situation where their responses to a particular event could be unobtrusively observed and recorded. In the case of children, researchers with access to school populations were sometimes able to conduct investigations of children without their knowledge or their parents' knowledge. In such cases, the subjects of the research neither were aware of their participation nor had agreed to be studied.

Recently, psychologists have become aware of the potential invasions of privacy that could occur under such circumstances and have instituted a requirement of *informed consent*. That is, subjects are advised in advance of the general nature of the study and are asked to give their written permission to participate. This procedure gives subjects the option of declining to participate before information about them is collected. In the case of research with children, parents now typically are required to consent in writing before their children become subjects of a research investigation. At times, the school may obtain a general permission from the parents and then act *in loco parentis* (in the place of the parents) to determine in each case whether participation will be allowed.

It is more difficult to obtain clear consent from the subjects themselves when they are young children. Often we cannot be certain that a child's willingness to participate in an experiment indicates an actual awareness of the implications of this action. For this reason, the right of *dissent* must be respected by the child researcher. That is, even if a child previously agreed to participate, his or her refusal to continue should be permitted without coercion or threat.

A related issue involves confidentiality. Although a subject agrees to be studied, the use and availability of the data may present additional questions. For example, a psychologist studying parent-child interactions may gather considerable information regarding the parents' attitudes, child-rearing practices, marital interactions, and so on. This information may be crucial to the research questions under investigation, but it may be considered quite personal from the parents' point of view. If the psychologist were to publish the results of this research, the issue of confidentiality might certainly arise.

In such cases, most psychologists attempt to maintain *subject anonymity* when reporting their findings. Sometimes this is accomplished by simply reporting group data (mean scores or combined results). In other situations, such as individual case studies, it may be necessary to disguise the identity of the subjects by reporting only the information that is relevant to the research question (such as age or sex). This practice probably benefits the researcher as well as the subject, since many more people may be willing to cooperate in psychological investigations under these conditions.

Nontreated Controls

Another type of ethical issue arises primarily in clinical or applied research. Many studies are designed to examine the potential effectiveness of a new treatment, therapy technique, or teaching method. To evaluate a new method, psychologists often retain one group of subjects as an untreated control population while the experimental subjects receive the treatment under study. Then any subsequent improvement in the performance of the experimental group can be compared with the performance of the control group.

If the treatment proves effective, an ethical question arises: Should the psychologist be content with having confirmed the value of the new treatment, or is there an obligation to apply the treatment to the nontreated control subjects? Psychologists are now of the opinion that control subjects should not be left untreated if an effective therapy method has been demonstrated. This requirement frequently can provide more to the psychologist than simply extra work, however; it also provides an opportunity for replication of the findings of the original research.

Besides using this procedure, it is also possible to use certain experimental designs that do not require untreated control subjects. The *changing-criterion design* and the *multiple-baseline across subjects* (discussed in Chapter 6) each provides for demonstration of functional relationships between treatments and target behaviors by applying the treatment procedures to all subjects, but in a somewhat piecemeal or staggered fashion. At the end of the intervention procedures, all subjects have received the same treatment methods or therapy techniques, thereby eliminating the problem of untreated subjects.

Social Ramifications

A final ethical consideration involves the interpretation and implications of research findings. Science strives to be objective. The ultimate goal is to acquire knowledge and understand the world as it exists—not necessarily as we expect it or would like it to exist, but as it actually is. Scientific research is always conducted within a social and political atmosphere, however. Sometimes, in the quest for knowledge, the scientist's findings may generate important and perhaps disturbing implications for social policy issues.

A good example of this situation is recent research involving heredity and intelligence. There has been a long-standing debate as to whether intelligence is primarily inherited or is a result of the child's environment and experiences. Related to this question is the question of whether environmental intervention can be effective in preventing or raising lower levels of intellectual ability.

Many researchers have attempted to address this issue from a purely scientific point of view. However, the findings in this area often become immediately relevant to major political and economic policy decisions. For example, the federal government has spent large sums of money to finance such programs as Project Head Start or Follow Through. These programs are based in part on the presumption that intellectual abilities are capable of improvement by environmental intervention. There is considerable evidence on both sides of this issue, however, and well-respected scientists disagree on the meaning of the data. Policy-makers who hold a position on this issue, however, may be quick to point out a particular investigator's findings to support their own cause. For this reason, some people have suggested that research on this issue be suspended entirely.

It becomes possible, therefore, for the purely objective scientist to be faced with a serious ethical dilemma. The researcher may produce evidence that supports one or the other position (only at some acceptable level of uncertainty, of course), but the scientist may not be prepared to have social policy based only on these findings. To report them, however, may provide necessary fuel for one political side and may inaccurately portray the scientist as a spokesperson for the position. But to withhold the results would be to conceal legitimately obtained scientific data, which may be of value to other researchers.

It is, perhaps, easiest to adopt the position that the scientist's first obligation should be to knowledge and truth, and that sociopolitical considerations ought not enter into this process. But, more and more, psychologists seem to be acknowledging that the very same data may have vastly different societal impact, depending on the particular climate in which they are reported. This has led to a greater awareness of this issue and the scientist's larger role in society. No simple solution exists to this problem. One writer, however, has suggested that scientists should be free to investigate and report on whatever areas they like, but they must also accept some of the social responsibility for their reports (Cronbach, 1975).

FIGURE 11.1
Testing and experimentation are conducted to answer scientific questions, but the nature of the research may also raise important ethical and social issues.

Conclusion

In this chapter we have examined some of the potential ethical issues and have suggested several solutions. But, to some degree, we have presented only one side of the issue. A competing argument holds that the ultimate fruits of research will benefit all of us. Therefore, some amount of risk may be worth the eventual progress we achieve.

This argument, of course, is extremely difficult to settle, because we cannot easily weigh the amount of current risks against the yet-undiscovered benefits. And even if this were possible, the amount of risk we should be willing to accept is far from obvious. Another factor that enters into this question involves the ease with which alternative methods are available. Certainly we would all agree that a no-risk method producing the same information would be preferable to one involving any amount of risk. But when no reasonable alternative exists, we must decide how important the scientific knowledge might be, compared with the potential harm the research may cause.

The sensitive nature of these issues has led researchers to make many of these decisions as a group. In some research situations, scientists have established *peer review* procedures, which are enacted before carrying out their investigations. In this way, other scientists are asked to consider the research methods with regard to potential risks, necessity for deception, nature of debriefing, and other ethical issues. Combining judgments in this way does not necessarily guarantee more ethical decisions, but it may serve, at a minimum, to keep scientists continually alert to many of these ethical issues. Table 11.1 summarizes the current ethical standards for research with children, as developed by the *Society for Research in Child Development*.

TABLE 11.1
Ethical Standards for Research with Children Developed by The Society for Research in Child Development

Children as research subjects present ethical problems for the investigator different from those presented by adult subjects. Not only are children often viewed as more vulnerable to stress but, having less knowledge and experience, they are less able to evaluate what participation in research may mean. Consent of the parent for the study of his child, moreover, must be obtained in addition to the child's consent. These are some of the major differences between research with children and research with adults.

1. No matter how young the child, he has rights that supersede the rights of the investigator. The investigator should measure each operation he proposes in terms of the child's rights, and before proceeding he should obtain the approval of a committee of peers. Institutional peer review committees should be established in any setting where children are the subjects of the study.

2. The final responsibility to establish and maintain ethical practices in research remains with the individual investigator. He is also responsible for the ethical practices of collaborators, assistants, students, and employees, all of whom, however, incur parallel obligations.

TABLE 11.1 *(continued)*

3. Any deviation from the following principles demands that the investigator seek consultation on the ethical issues in order to protect the rights of the research participants.

4. The investigator should inform the child of all features of the research that may affect his willingness to participate and he should answer the child's questions in terms appropriate to the child's comprehension.

5. The investigator should respect the child's freedom to choose to participate in research or not, as well as to discontinue participation at any time. The greater the power of the investigator with respect to the participant, the greater is the obligation to protect the child's freedom.

6. The informed consent of parents or of those who act *in loco parentis* (e.g., teachers, superintendents of institutions) similarly should be obtained, preferably in writing. Informed consent requires that the parent or other responsible adult be told all features of the research that may affect his willingness to allow the child to participate. This information should include the profession and institutional affiliation of the investigator. Not only should the right of the responsible adult to refuse consent be respected, but he should be given the opportunity to refuse without penalty.

7. The informed consent of any person whose interaction with the child is the subject of the study should also be obtained. As with the child and responsible adult, informed consent requires that the person be informed of all features of the research that may affect his willingness to participate; his questions should be answered; and he should be free to choose to participate or not, and to discontinue participation at any time.

8. From the beginning of each research investigation, there should be a clear agreement between the investigator and the research participant that defines the responsibilities of each. The investigator has the obligation to honor all promises and commitments of the agreement.

9. The investigator uses no research operation that may harm the child either physically or psychologically. Psychological harm, to be sure, is difficult to define; nevertheless, its definition remains the responsibility of the investigator. When the investigator is in doubt about the possible harmful effects of the research operations, he seeks consultation from others. When harm seems possible, he is obligated to find other means of obtaining the information or to abandon the research.

10. Although we accept the ethical ideal of full disclosure of information, a particular study may necessitate concealment or deception. Whenever concealment or deception is thought to be essential to the conduct of the study, the investigator should satisfy a committee of his peers that his judgment is correct. If concealment or deception is practiced, adequate measures should be taken after the study to ensure the participant's understanding of the reasons for the concealment or deception.

11. The investigator should keep in confidence all information obtained about research participants. The participant's identity should be concealed in written and verbal reports of the results, as well as in informal discussions with students and colleagues. When a possibility exists that others may gain access to such information, this possibility, together with the plans for protecting confidentiality, should be explained to the participants as a part of the procedure of obtaining informed consent.

12. To gain access to institutional records, the investigator should obtain permission from responsible individuals or authorities in charge of records. He should preserve the anonymity of the information and extract no informa-

TABLE 11.1 *(continued)*

tion other than that for which permission was obtained. It is the investigator's responsibility to insure that these authorities do, in fact, have the confidence of the subject and that they bear some degree of responsibility in giving such permission.

13. Immediately after the data are collected, the investigator should clarify for the research participant any misconceptions that may have arisen. The investigator also recognizes a duty to report general findings to participants in terms appropriate to their understanding. Where scientific or humane values may justify withholding information, every effort should be made so that withholding the information has no damaging consequences for the participant.

14. Because the investigator's words may carry unintended weight with parents and children, caution should be exercised in reporting results, making evaluative statements, or giving advice.

15. When, in the course of research, information comes to the investigator's attention that may seriously affect the child's well-being, the investigator has a responsibility to discuss the information with those expert in the field in order that the parents may arrange the necessary assistance for their child.

16. When research procedures may result in undesirable consequences for the participant that were previously unforeseen, the investigator should employ appropriate measures to correct these consequences, and should consider redesigning the procedures.

17. The investigator should be mindful of the social, political, and human implications of his research and should be especially careful in the presentation of his findings. This standard, however, in no way denies the investigator the right to pursue any area of research or the right to observe proper standards of scientific reporting.

18. When an experimental treatment under investigation is believed to be of benefit to children, control groups should be offered other beneficial alternative treatments, if available, instead of no treatment.

19. Teachers of courses related to children should demonstrate their concern for the rights of research participants by presenting these ethical standards to their students so that from the outset of training the participants' rights are regarded as important as substantive findings and experimental design.

20. Every investigator has a responsibility to maintain not only his own ethical standards but also those of his colleagues.

21. Editors of journals reporting investigations of children have certain responsibilities to the authors of studies they review: they should provide space where necessary for the investigator to justify his procedures and to report the precautions he has taken. When the procedures seem questionable, editors should ask for such information.

22. The Society and its members have a continuing responsibility to question, amend, and revise these standards.

References

Baumrind, D. Informed consent and deceit in research with children and their parents. Paper presented at the meeting of the *Society for Research in Child Development*, New Orleans, 1977.

Cronbach, L. J. Five decades of public controversy over mental testing. *American Psychologist*, 1975, **30**, 1–14.

Dennis, W. Infant development under conditions of restricted practice and of minimum social stimulation. *Genetic Psychology Monographs*, 1941, **23**, 143–189.

Smith, M. B. Conflicting values affecting behavioral research with children. *Children*, 1967, **4**, 377–382.

Watson, J. B., and Raynor, R. Conditioned emotional reactions. *Journal of Experimental Psychology*, 1920, **3**, 1–14.

12 Scientific Communication

This final chapter will be devoted to a brief consideration of child research as a professional enterprise. We have discussed research methods and techniques at some length, but it is often not clear precisely who conducts this research and how one goes about reporting it. In addition, the sources of research articles and their general format also warrant some discussion.

Research Settings

Most research with children is conducted at colleges and universities. Academic psychologists frequently maintain on-going research programs as part of their professional obligations. In addition, graduate students in doctoral programs typically are required to conduct research projects as part of their training, which, of course, culminates in their doctoral dissertation research. Occasionally, M.A. candidates and undergraduates also produce research results that eventually reach publication. Some child research is also conducted within hospital settings, often as part of a medical school program. Most often, these investigations involve newborns or are concerned with clinically related issues. A few institutions, such as the National Institute of Mental Health, are devoted solely to research, some of which involves children. Finally, and to a lesser degree, research with children is conducted by individuals affiliated with elementary schools, daycare centers, residential treatment centers for exceptional children, and psychologists in private practice.

Professional Societies

One method of disseminating research findings is through professional organizations formed by psychologists and other researchers for this purpose. The major organization of psychologists is the *American Psychological Association (APA)*. This group is composed of members from all areas of psychology, but it is subdivided into various specialty divisions. Most child researchers in this organization are affiliated with the Developmental Psychology subgroup (Division 7), although several other divisions also include child researchers. A second professional group concerned exclusively with children is the *Society for Research in Child Development (SRCD)*. This organization is the most important and prestigious of its kind and its members represent the leading child researchers in the world. Other societies interested in child research include the *American Educational Research Association (AERA)* and the *Society for the Experimental Analysis of Behavior.*

One important role of these societies is the sponsoring of periodic conferences to discuss recent research findings and to debate important issues. The *APA* holds a major national convention each year for this purpose, and it also sponsors regional conventions, which are smaller and somewhat more informal. *SRCD* hosts a major convention biannually, with regional conferences held each year in different parts of the country.

Professional Journals

The principal method of communicating research findings and ideas to the scientific community is through professional journals. When an investigator has generated some results that may be of value to others or that shed light on an important issue, the findings may be set down in a research article and submitted to a professional journal. The editors of the journal then evaluate the article, often by seeking the opinions of other researchers in that specific area, and the editors either accept it for publication or decline it. The principal bases for such decisions involve the methodological quality of the work and the importance of the findings.

Some journals are rather general in their contents, whereas others focus on more specific topics or methods. In child-research, there are a number of prominent journals, which we shall describe briefly.

Developmental Psychology. This journal is published by the *APA* and includes research reports and theoretical articles on any area of developmental research. All ages are permissible, from prenatal studies to gerontology (study of aging). Nonhuman research is also permitted, as long as it addresses a developmental issue.

Child Development. This journal is published by *SRCD*. It focuses exclusively on research with children, including both the results of specific investigations and more general reviews of the literature on a particular topic. Both experimental and nonexperimental research are permissible.

Journal of Experimental Child Psychology. This journal is devoted exclusively to research with children conducted within an experimental design. Correlational studies are not included. Most of these articles involve laboratory rather than field investigations and are usually of a very high quality.

Journal of Applied Behavior Analysis. This journal is devoted to the application of psychological principles and techniques to problems of social importance. Studies involving children are often set in classroom situations or involve clinical intervention programs in the home or in institutional settings. These studies typically involve time-series research designs (see Chapter 6) rather than between-subjects experiments (see Chapter 5).

Journal of Educational Psychology. Most of the articles appearing in this *APA* journal are concerned with research involving teaching and learning principles. The studies are not necessarily all of the applied variety, but include many basic investigations into the fundamental psychological processes related to learning.

Many other professional journals also publish articles involving research with children. Some of these include: *Human Development, Journal of Personality and Social Psychology, Journal of Genetic Psychology, Merrill-Palmer Quarterly of Behavior and Development, Infant Behavior and Development, Journal of Abnormal Child Psychology,* and *Journal of School Psychology.*

Journal Format

The research article, as presented in most journals, is prepared according to a specific format. The reader who has not had experience with actual primary-source readings may find an outline of this format useful.

Introduction

Each article begins by presenting the theoretical and historical context of the research. Why was this study conducted? What related research has already been done? What issues need attention or clarification? Often the introduction section ends with a specific set of predictions—that is, the experimental hypotheses are enumerated.

Method

In this section the actual details of the investigation are described. These include a description of the subjects and setting, details of any specific stimuli or apparatus involved, and a careful account of the precise procedures to which each subject was exposed. The crucial element of the method section is that the information must be presented in sufficient detail so that a researcher who reads the article could actually replicate the experiment.

Results

The actual findings of the investigation are presented next, along with the appropriate statistical analyses. Often the data are presented in tables or graphs to allow visual examination of the results. In this section, the researcher does not attempt to interpret or discuss the meaning of the findings. That function is reserved until the final section.

Discussion

Once the data have been presented and the analyses described, the investigator is free to comment on their meaning. Often the discussion relates the findings to the initial predictions, with the author attempting to resolve any discrepancies. The value of the results for larger issues or theories is frequently considered at this point, along with potential future research questions that may now be apparent. This section is where the greatest amount of speculation and informal theorizing generally occurs.

Abstract

Most journals also require a one-hundred to two-hundred word summary of the study. This includes a brief statement of intent, procedures, and results. Frequently, the abstract is presented at the beginning of the article to give the reader an opportunity to quickly scan the general nature of the research. Abstracts are also published separately in some sources to facilitate literature searches and reviews.

Conclusion

We have focused in this last chapter on several professional aspects of research with children. It is appropriate that we conclude our presentation with this information, because it represents a vital link in the entire research process. If the information obtained in research investigations is not communicated adequately, its value may remain unappreciated and the rate of scientific progress greatly diminished.

It is our hope that, after having completed this text, the reader will be a major step closer to understanding the research enterprise at all phases—from theoretical assumptions, through research design and methodology, to the communication of the results. We have presented many important issues and concepts at an elementary level of sophistication, leaving in-depth coverage to advanced courses and readings. Whether as an actual researcher or as a consumer of research findings, we believe that the reader should now be in a better position to understand and evaluate the challenging and fascinating process of studying children.

Name Index

Adams, H. E., 182
Ainsworth, M. D. S., 41, 47
Asher, S. R., 136, 138

Baer, D. M., 91, 100, 130, 132,
    133, 138, 170, 182
Ball, W., 154, 156
Baltes, P. B., 25, 31, 36, 47
Bandura, A., 104, 105, 117
Barker, R. G., 167, 181
Barkley, R. A., 132, 137
Barlow, D. H., 100
Barrett-Goldfarb, M. S.,
    155, 156
Bartoshuk, A. K., 142, 156
Baumrind, D., 190, 198
Beach, D. R., 107, 117
Becker, W. C., 171, 183
Bell, R. Q., 40, 47
Bellugi, U., 129, 138, 168, 181
Bloom, K., 107, 108, 111, 117
Bloom, L. M., 168, 181
Bower, T. G. R., 148, 149,
    155, 156
Bowlby, J., 41, 47
Bradley, R., 35, 47
Braine, M. D. S., 168, 181
Brecht, J. M., 132, 137

Bridger, W. H., 142, 156
Brown, A. L., 120, 121, 122, 137
Brown, C. J., 145, 146, 157
Brown, R. W., 129, 138
    168, 181
Bruno, L. A., 141, 142, 157
Burger, G., 166, 181

Caldwell, B. M., 35, 47, 169, 182
Calhoun, K. S., 182
Campbell, D. T., 17, 31
Campos, J. J., 153, 156
Cazden, C. B., 129, 130, 138,
    168, 181
Chinsky, J. M., 107, 177
Church, J., 163, 181
Ciminero, A. R., 182
Cooley, J. A., 152, 158
Corl, K. G., 39, 47
Cronbach, L. J., 194, 199

Darwin, C., 163, 181
Dennis, W., 183, 187, 199
Denny, N. W., 127, 128,
    129, 138
Diament, C., 178, 182
Dickson, W. J., 27, 31
Dietz, A., 178, 182

Dirks, J., 135, 136, 138
Drabman, R. S., 116, 117
Duchnowski, A. J., 132, 138

Ebbesen, E. B., 114, 116, 117
Eimas, P. D., 143, 156
Emerson, P. E., 165, 182
Engen, T., 142, 156
Esposito, A., 107, 108, 111, 117

Fagan, J. F., 146, 147, 156
Fagen, J. W., 152, 157
Flavell, J. H., 107, 117
Foster, S. L., 175, 180, 182
Frankel, G. W., 115, 118
Friedlander, B. Z., 155, 157
Friedman, S., 141, 142, 157

Gelman, R., 168, 182
Gesell, A., 53, 65
Gewirtz, J. L., 132, 133, 138
Gibson, E. J., 153, 157
Goetz, E. M., 130, 131, 138
Gordon, I. J., 155, 157
Greene, D., 45, 57
Gump, P. V., 40, 47

Haaf, R. A., 145, 146, 157
Hale, G. A., 120, 123, 138
Hall, R. V., 95, 100
Harlow, H. F., 52, 65
Hartmann, D. P., 95, 100,
    175, 182
Hartup, W. W., 118, 134
Hersher, L., 169, 182
Herson, M., 100
Hetherington, E. M., 47
Hill, J. P., 138

Jusczyk, P., 143, 156

Kagan, J., 37, 47, 113, 118
Kanowitz, J., 179, 182
Kazdin, A. E., 99, 100
Kent, R. N., 175, 178, 179,
    180, 182

Kessen, M. L., 145, 157
Kessen, W., 145, 157
Klein, R. E., 37, 47
Kotelchuck, M., 113, 118
Kuypers, D. S., 171, 183

Langer, A., 153, 156
Leopold, W., 168, 182
Lepper, M. R., 45, 47
Lerner, M. J., 19, 31
Lipsitt, L. P., 34, 47, 140, 142,
    155, 156, 157, 158
Lipton, E. L., 169, 182
Long, G. T., 19, 31

McElwee, J. D., 180, 182
McGraw, M. B., 53, 65
McKirdy, L. S., 152, 157
Mash, E. J., 180, 182
Milewski, A. E., 143, 157
Mischel, W., 114, 116, 117
Moore, B. S., 111, 117
Morse, P. A., 143, 157
Munroe, R. H., 37, 47
Munroe, R. L., 37, 47
Munsinger, H., 145, 157
Murphy, M. D., 120, 121,
    122, 137

Neisser, U., 135, 136, 138
Nesselroade, J. R., 36, 47
Nielsen, L. J., 171, 183
Nisbett, R. E., 45, 47
Novak, G., 109, 118
Nunnally, J. C., 132, 138

Oden, S., 136, 138
O'Leary, K. D., 178, 182
Otto, L., 132, 137

Parke, R. D., 47, 111, 112, 118
Parker, R. K., 132, 138
Patterson, G. R., 40, 47
Perloff, B., 104, 105, 117

Phillips, E. L., 105, 106, 117
Piaget, J., 164, 165
Pick, A. D., 115, 118
Piper, R. A., 120, 123, 138
Preyer, W., 163, 182

Raynor, R., 187, 199
Reese, H. W., 34, 36, 47,
    140, 158
Reid, J. B., 179, 182
Rheingold, H. L., 151, 152, 158
Richmond, J. B., 169, 182
Riddell, W. I., 39, 47
Risley, T. R., 91, 100
Roethlisberger, E. J., 27, 31
Rogers-Warren, A., 170, 182
Rosenhan, D. C., 111, 117
Rovee, C. K., 152, 157

Schaefer, E. S., 166, 182
Schaffer, H. R., 165, 182
Schaie, K. W., 25, 31
Shatz, M., 168, 182
Sidman, M., 83, 100
Siqueland, E. R., 143, 156, 157
Slaby, R. G., 111, 118
Slobin, D. I., 37, 47
Smith, M. B., 188, 199
Smothergill, N. L., 134
Spelke, E., 113, 118
Stanley, J. C., 17, 31
Stanley, W. C., 152, 158
Stern, G. G., 169, 182

Stevenson, H. W., 125
Suomi, S. J., 52, 65

Taplin, P. S., 179, 182
Thomas, D. A., 171, 175,
    176, 183
Thomas, H., 145, 158
Thomas, M. H., 116, 117
Thompson, H., 53, 65
Tiedemann, D., 163, 183
Tighe, L. S., 125, 138
Tighe, T. J., 125, 138
Trehub, S., 143, 144, 158
Tronick, E., 154, 156

Ullman, D. G., 132, 137
Underwood, B., 111, 117

Vasta, R., 126, 127, 138,
    140, 158
Vietze, P., 141, 142, 157
Vigorito, J., 143, 156

Walk, R. D., 153, 157
Watson, J. B., 187, 199
Weir, M. W., 133, 134, 135, 138
Whitehurst, G. J., 109, 110, 118,
    140, 155, 156, 158
Wolf, M. M., 91, 100
Wright, H. F., 167, 181

Zelazo, P., 113, 118
Zorn, G. A., 109, 118

Subject Index

Accuracy, 119–126
Analysis of variance, 76
Anonymity, subject, 192
Audition
    abilities in infants, 142–143
    preference in infants, 155

Baby biographies, 51–52, 163
Baseline, 85
Bias. *See also* Reactivity
    biasing influences, 21
    experimenter, 70–71, 179–180
    from historical events, 28–29,
        61–62
    from maturation, 28–29
    observer, 178–179
    obsolete data, 60, 62
    reactivity, 178, 180
    sampling, 21–25, 59

Changing-criterion design,
    95–96, 193
Choice, 131–135
Cohort effects, 23
Comparative research, 37–39
Complexity
    naive-sophisticated responses,
        126–129

repetitive-variable responses,
    129–131
Concept learning, 124–125
Conjugate reinforcement para-
    digm, 151–152
Constructs, 5–6, 11–12
Correlational studies, 53–58
Correlations, 54
Co-twin control, 53
Critical test, 43–44
Cross-cultural research, 36–37
Cumulative record, 109–110

Debriefing, 190
Dependent variable, 16
Depth perception
    impending collision, 154–155
    visual cliff, 152–153
Determinants of behavior
    current situational, 9
    historical, 8–9
    organismic, 9
Developmental research, 35–36
Duration, of behavior, 112–114

Ecological research, 39–41
Errors, nature of, 135
Ethological research, 41–42

Ethical standards of research with children, 196–198
Exploratory research, 45–46

Free classification studies, 127–129
Frequency, of behavior, 104–107
F test, 76
Functional analysis of behavior, 15–18

Graphing, 19, 110–111

Habituation-dishabituation paradigm, 140–142
Hawthorne effect, 27. *See also* Bias; Reactivity
Hypothesis, 4

Incidential learning paradigm, 120–123
Independent variable, 16, 19
Interaction effects, 79–80
Interval-sampling, 171
Interviewing parents, 165–166

Journal format, 203–204
Journals, professional, 201–203

Latency, of behavior, 114–116
Laws, 4
Longitudinal/cross-sectional design, 63

Magnitude, of behavior, 110–112
Matching problems, 126
Maturational factors, 28–29
Mean, 71
Memory abilities, 146–148. *See also* Recall
Mixed design, 81
Multiple-baseline design, 91–95, 191, 193
Multiple-factor designs, 77–81

Null hypothesis, 20, 44

Observations, types of
formal, 169–174
indirect, 165–166
informal, 163–165
stream of behavior, 166–168
Organizations, professional, 201

Paradigm, 119
Perceptual unity, in infants, 148–149
Physical harm to subjects, 188–190
Preference. *See* Choice
Privacy, violations of, 191–192
Probability learning problems, 133–135
Problem solving, 123–125
Psychological events, 7–8
Psychological harm to subjects, 188–190
Public events, 5

Quasi-experimental designs, 17, 57

Random assignment of subjects, 16–17, 68
Rate, of behavior, 107–110
Rating scales, 169–170
Raw scores, 71
Reactivity. *See also* Bias
Hawthorne effect, 27
repeated testing, 26–27, 60–61
subject awareness, 25–26
Recall
incidental learning, 120–123
central learning, 120
Reciprocal relationships, 40
Reductionism, 7–8
Reliability, of observations, 162, 175–177
Repeated-measures design, 76–77

Replication, 30
Research, dimensions of
  applied, 33–34
  basic, 33–34
  descriptive, 32–33
  manipulative, 32–33
Retrospective design, 63–64
Retrospective reports, 166
Reversal design, 86–91

Sampling, independent random,
  22–23
Satiation paradigm, 142–143
Scientific method, 3–4
Settings, for research, 200–201
Single-factor design, 75–77
Sociometric scores, 136–137
Standard deviation, 72
Subject selection
  control group, 27, 192–193
  experimental group, 27
  group versus individual study,
    97–98

matching, 67–68
random assignment, 16–17,
  68–69
Target behavior, 85, 170
Teleology, 8
Theories, use of in science, 4
Theory-testing, 12–14, 43–44
Time-sampling, 171–174
t test, 73–74
Two-factor design, 77–79

Variability, 30, 72
Vision
  discriminative abilities in in-
    fants, 140–141, 143–145
  preferences in infants,
    143–146

Withdrawal design, 86–91

Yoking procedures, 108